Flower Coloring Book by Dr. Deuce
Copyright © 2021 by Duke Jarboe. All rights reserved. No portion of this book, except for brief passages used in review, may be reproduced in any form without written permission by the publisher.

Published by Panda Publishing LLC
Cover design by Duke Jarboe
Created by Duke Jarboe

First Edition March 2021

Check out more books by Dr. Deuce! Scan the QR code below!

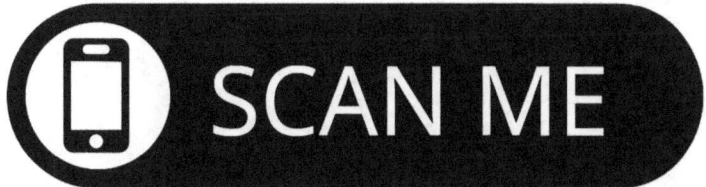

This Book Belongs to:

_____

_____

_____

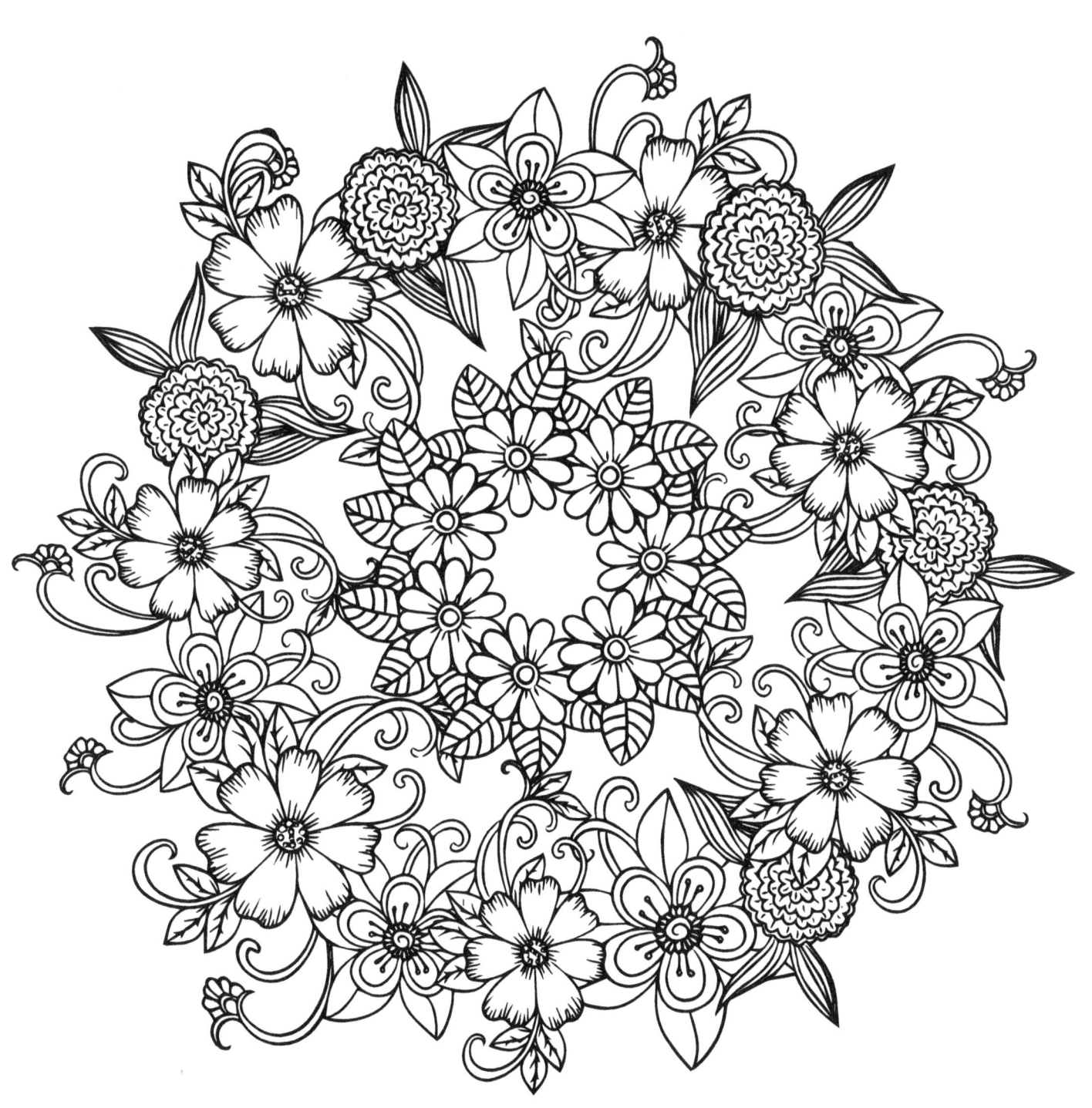

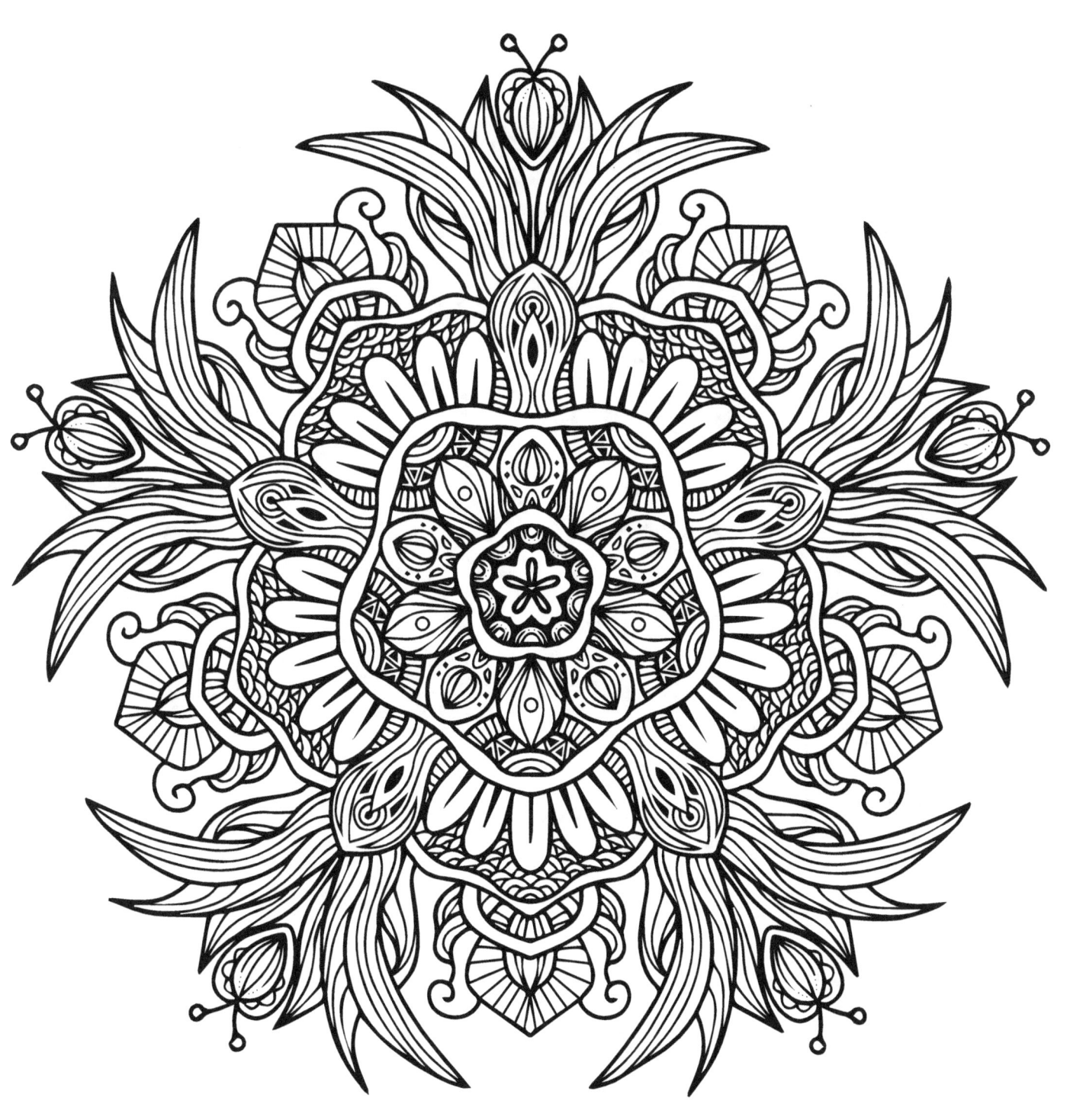

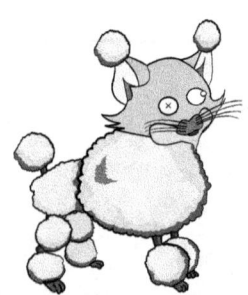

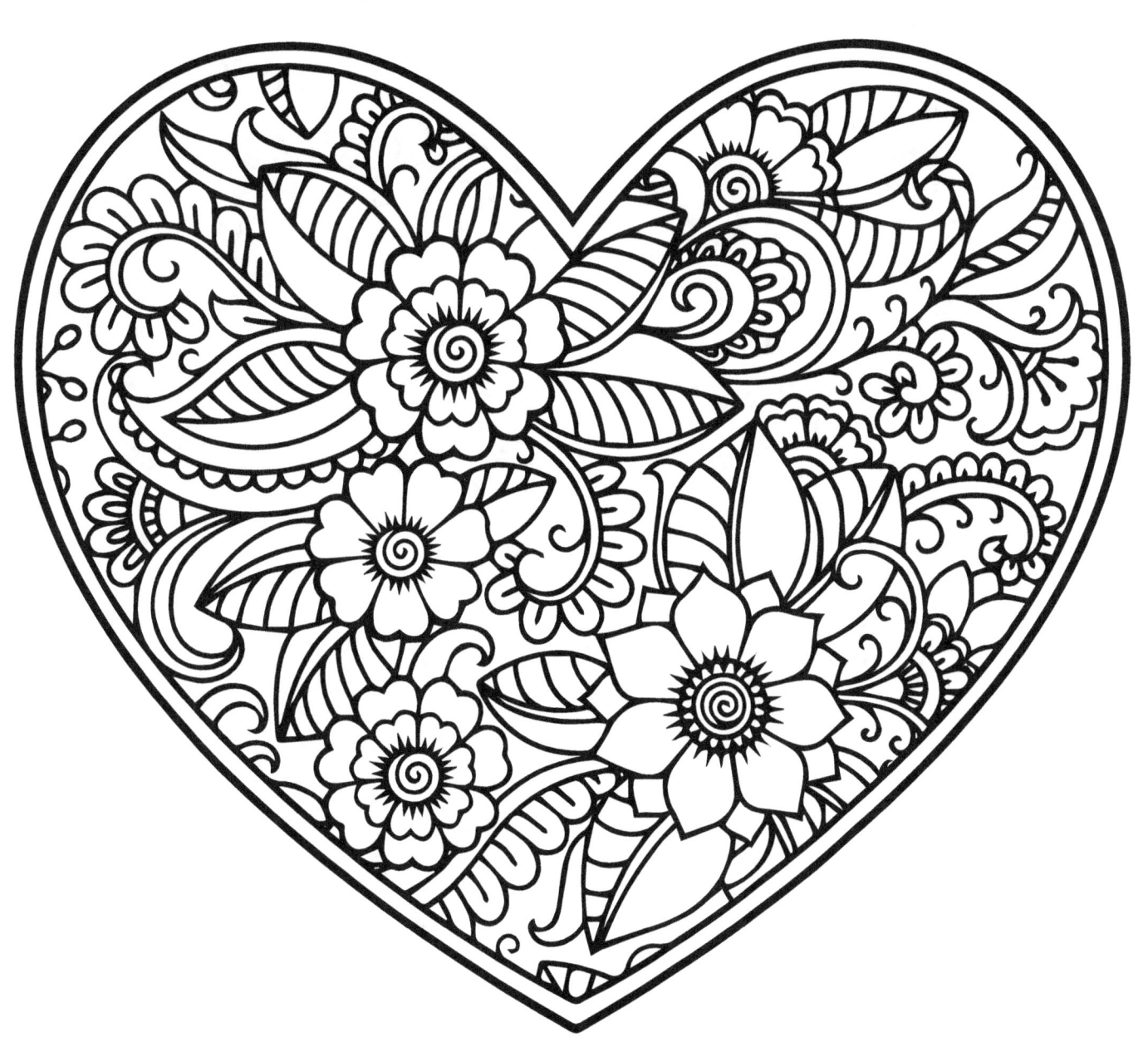

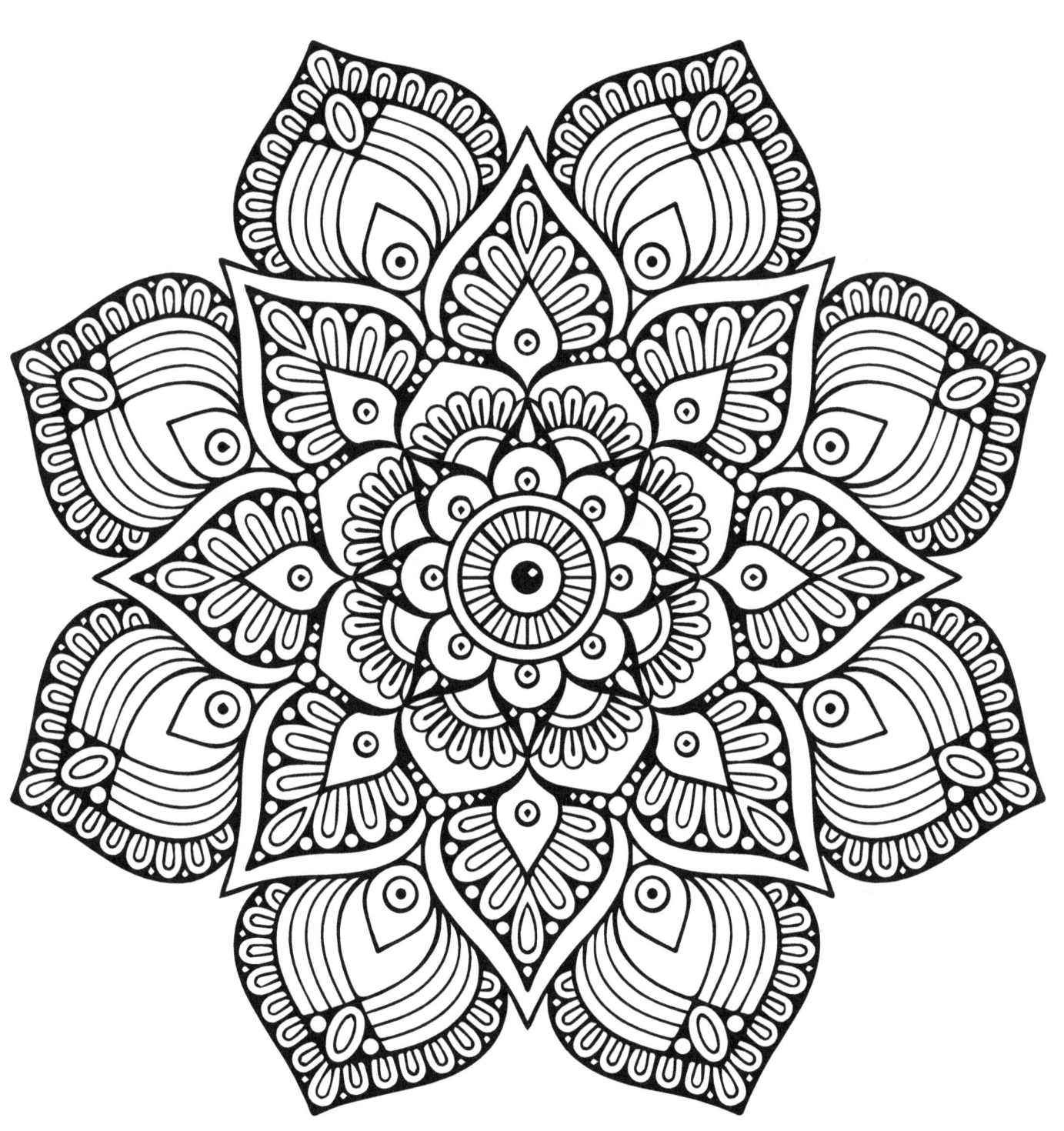

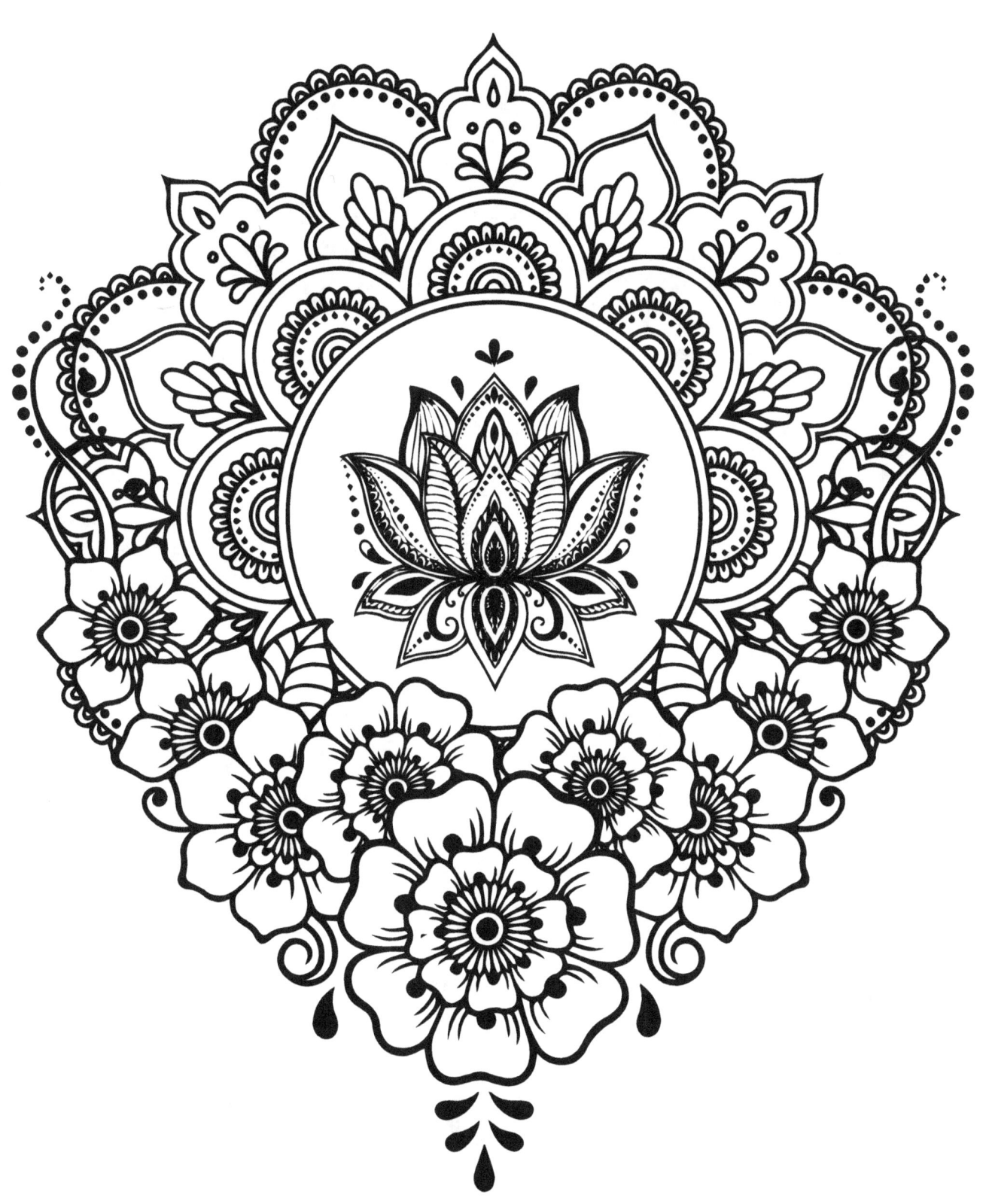

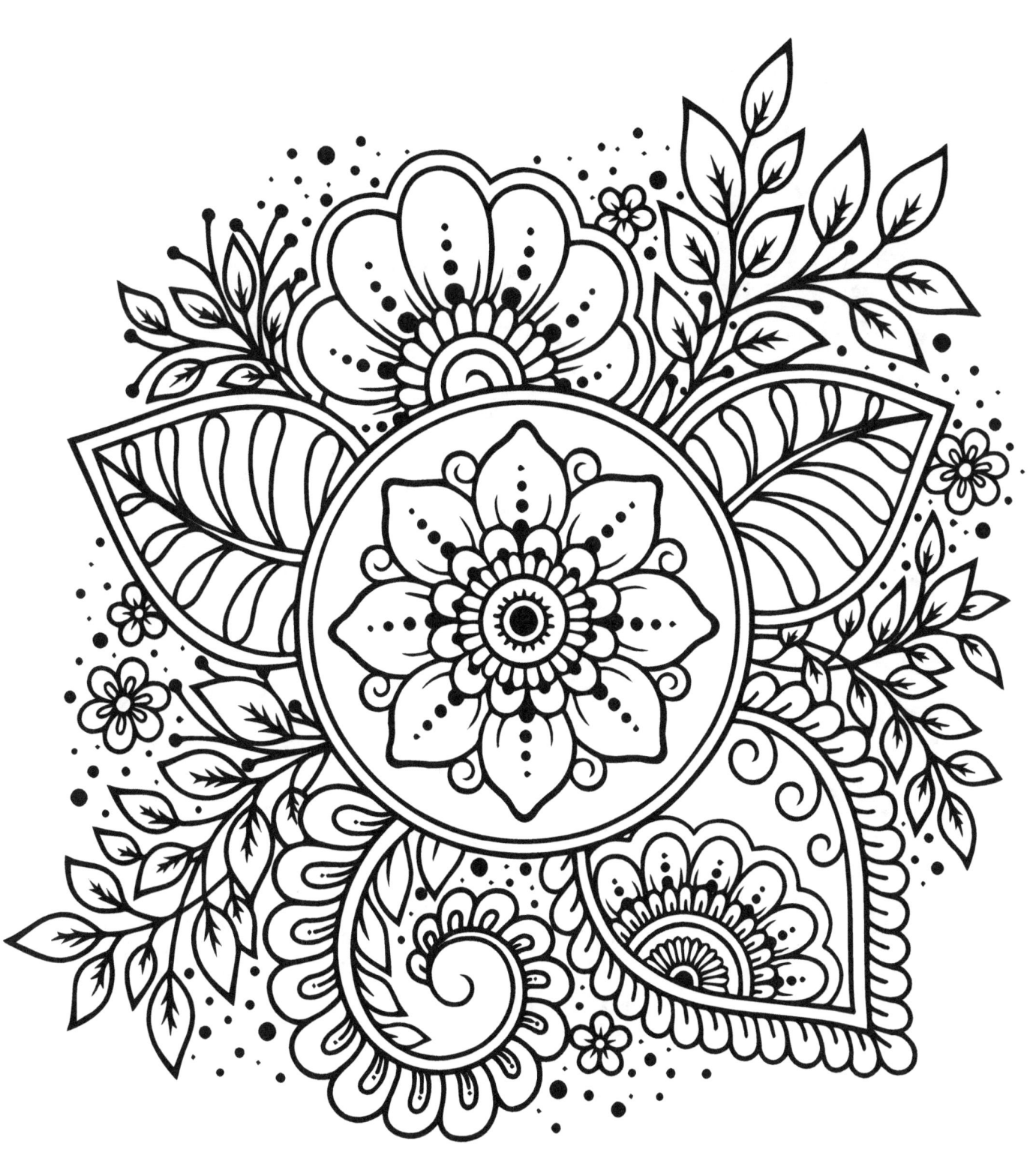

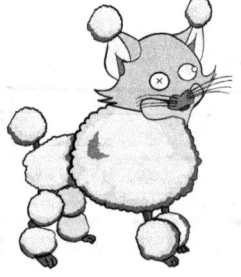

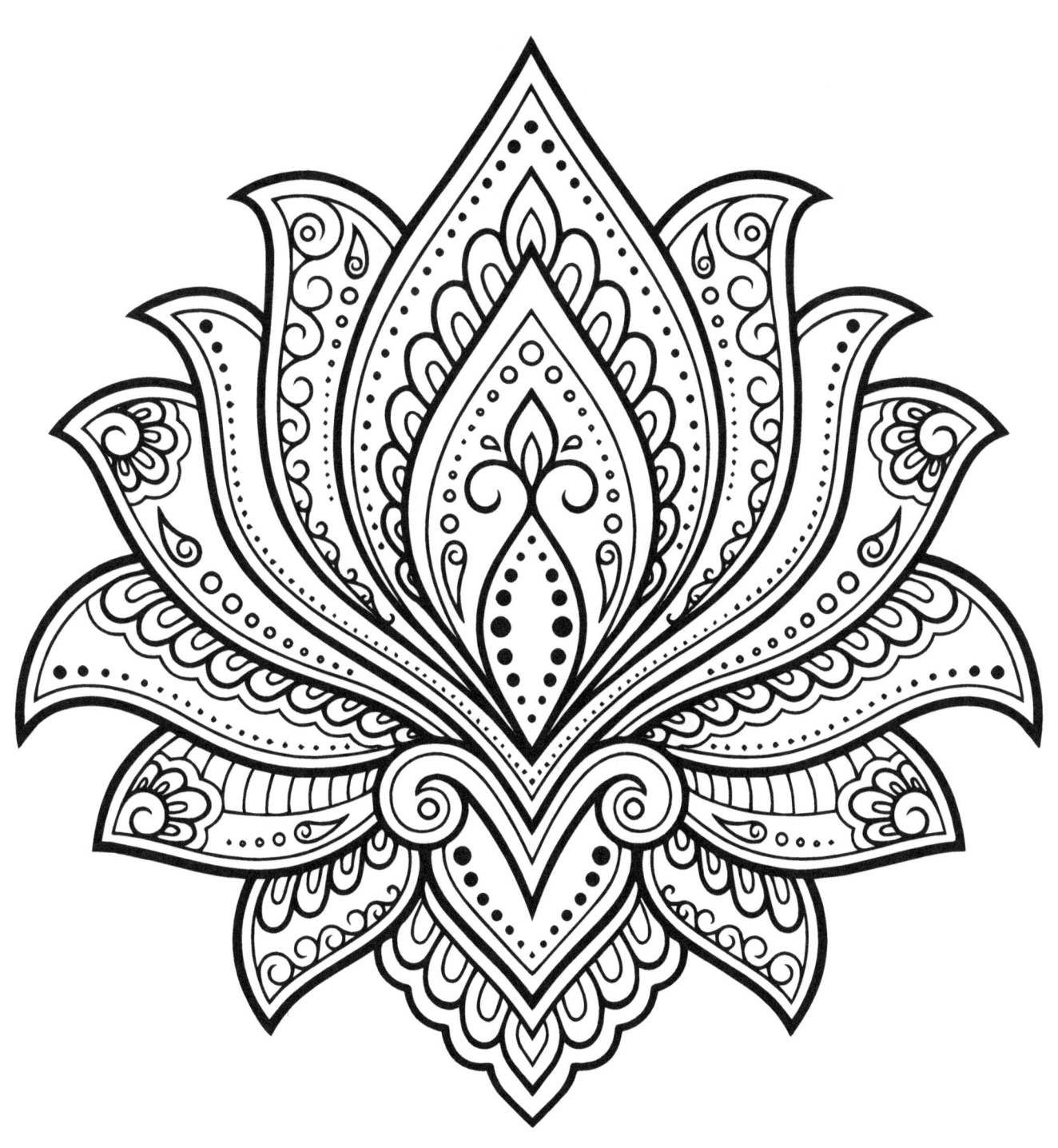

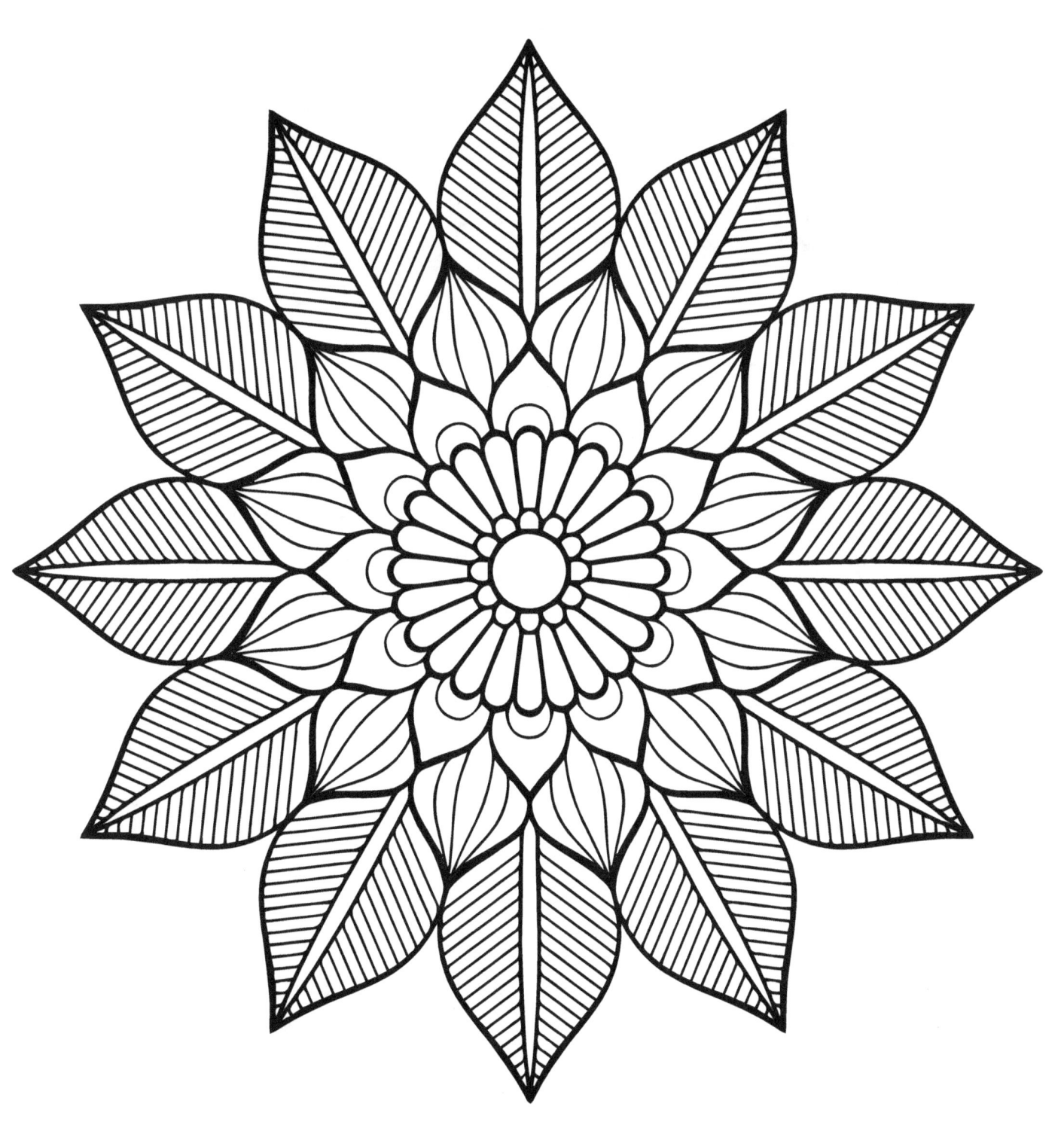

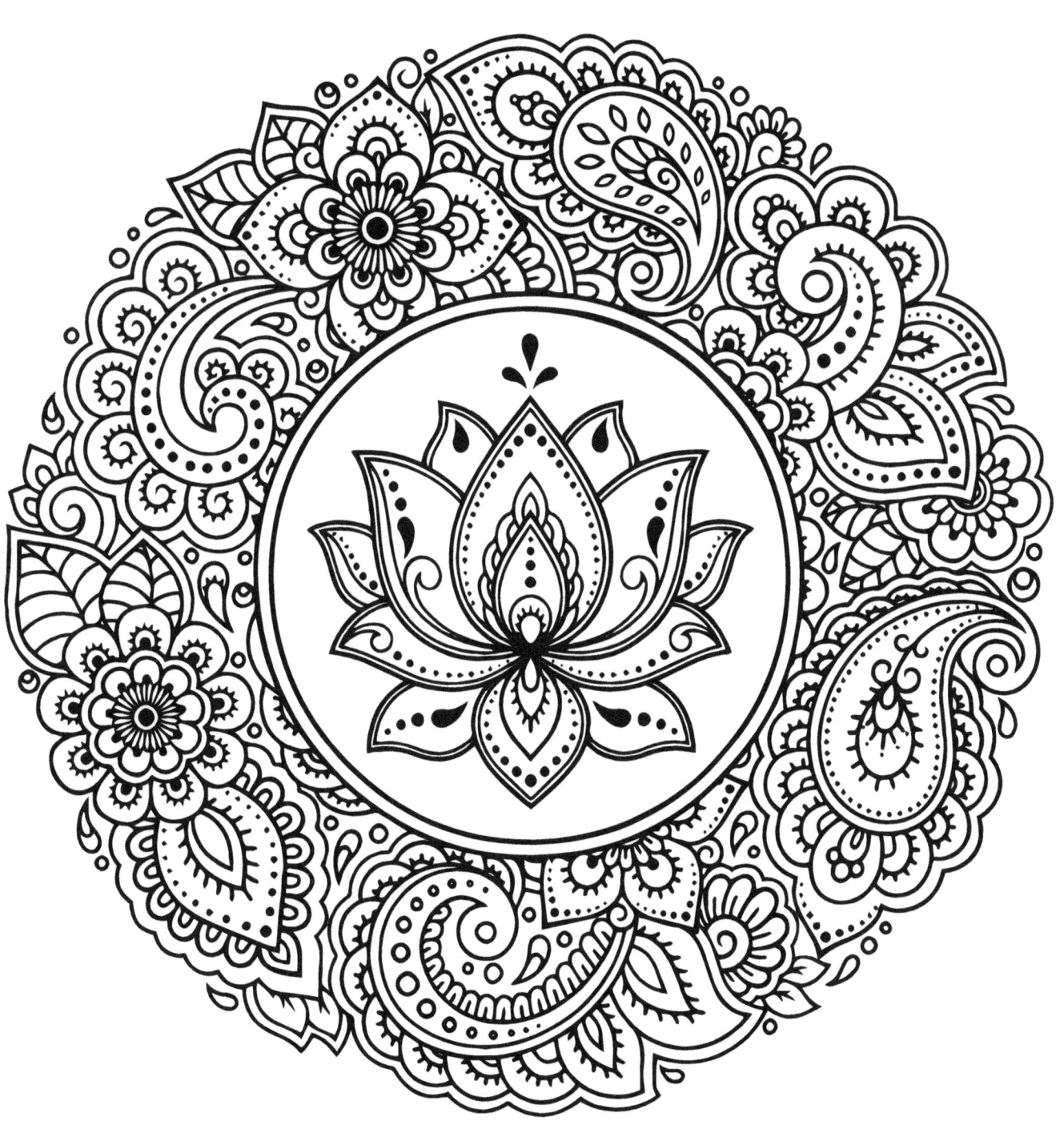

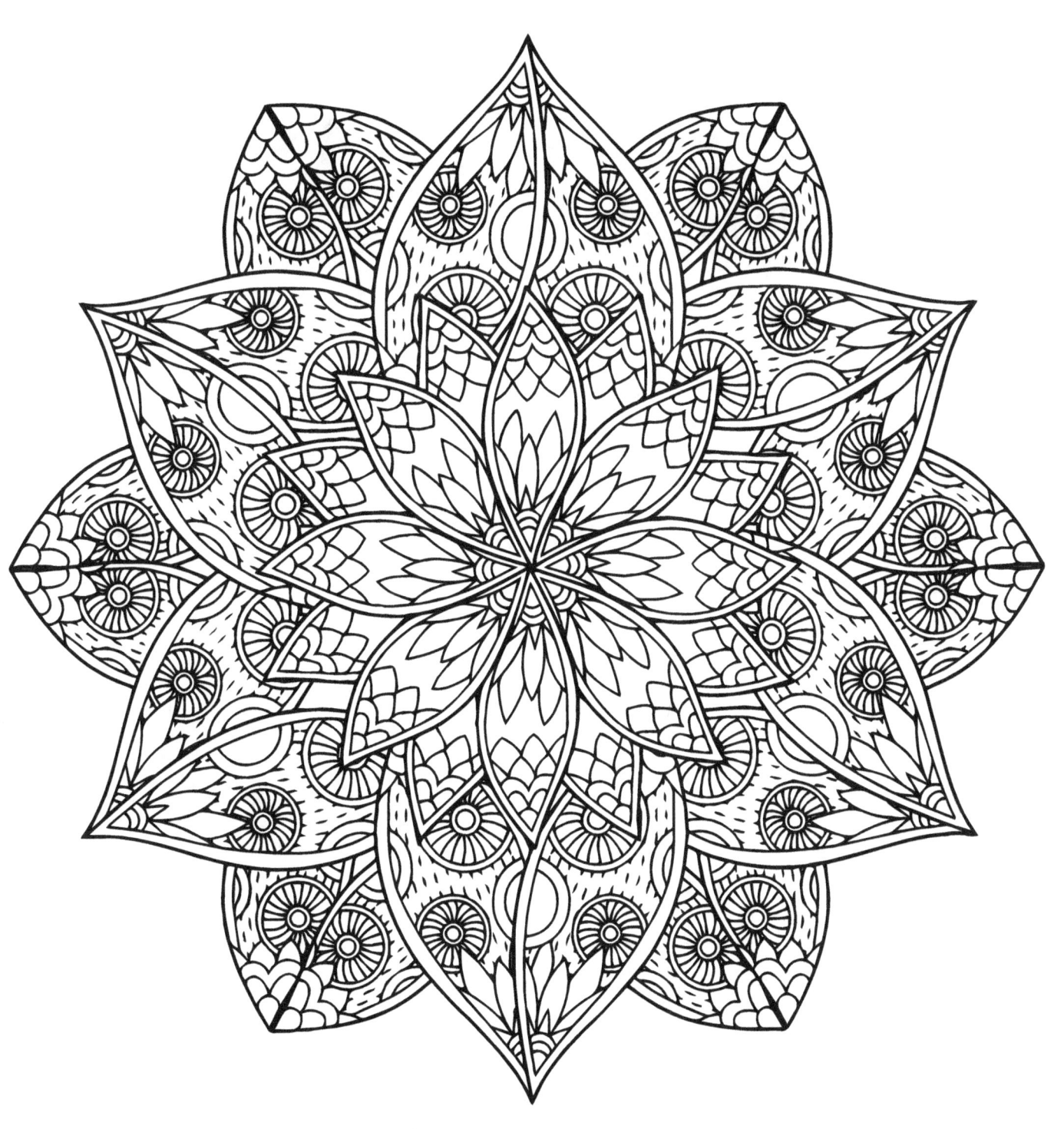

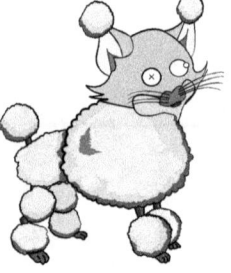

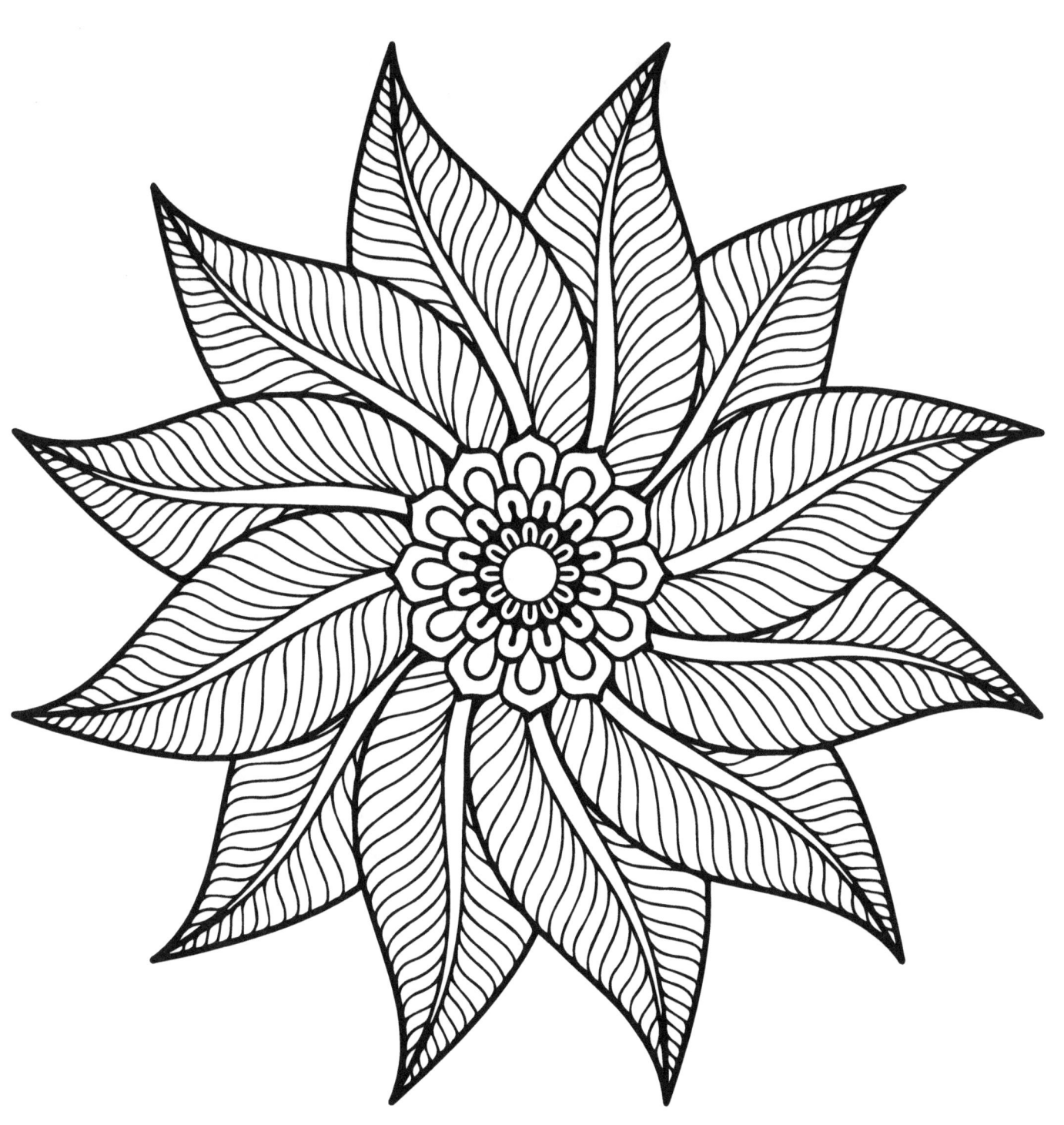

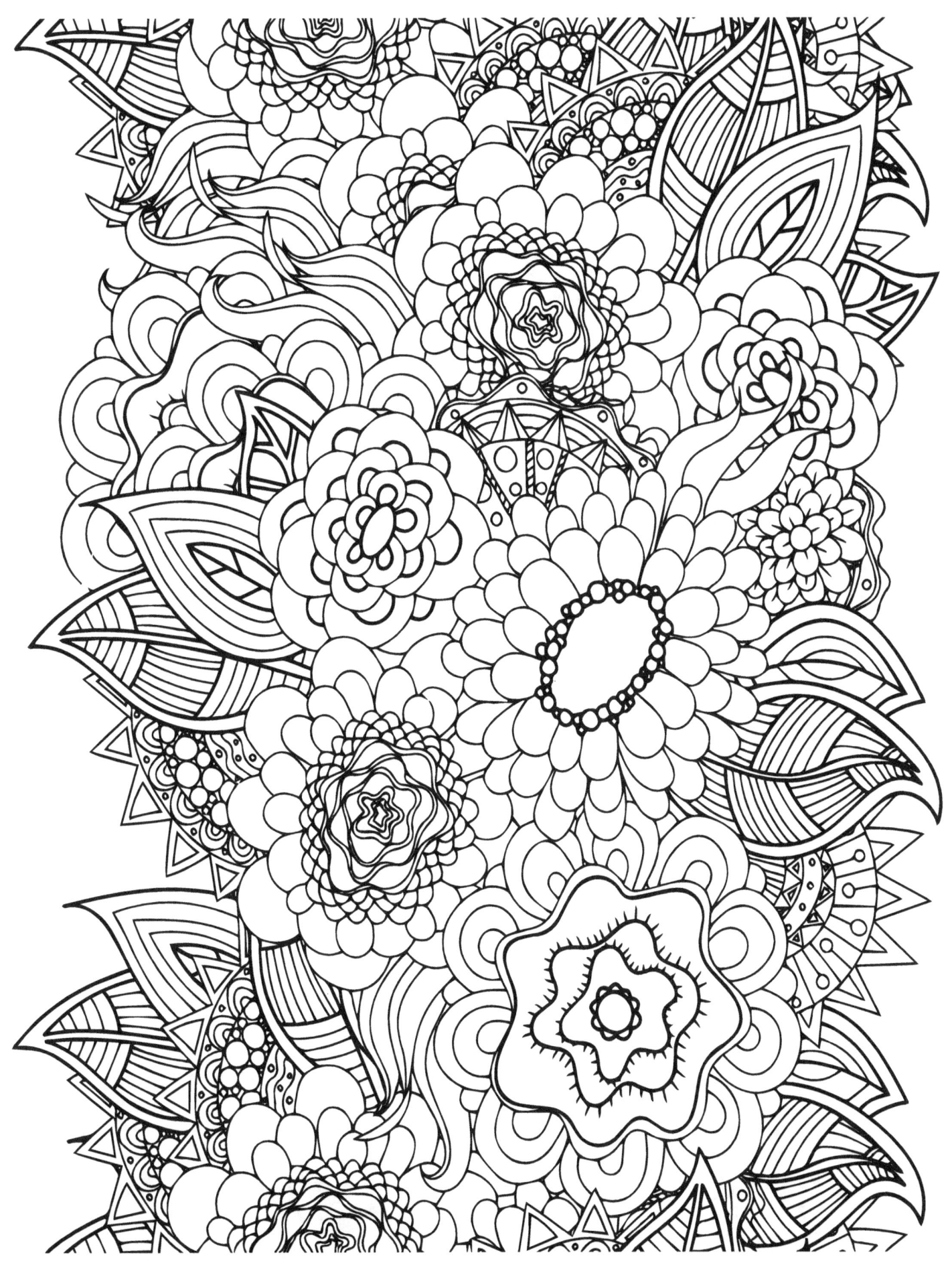

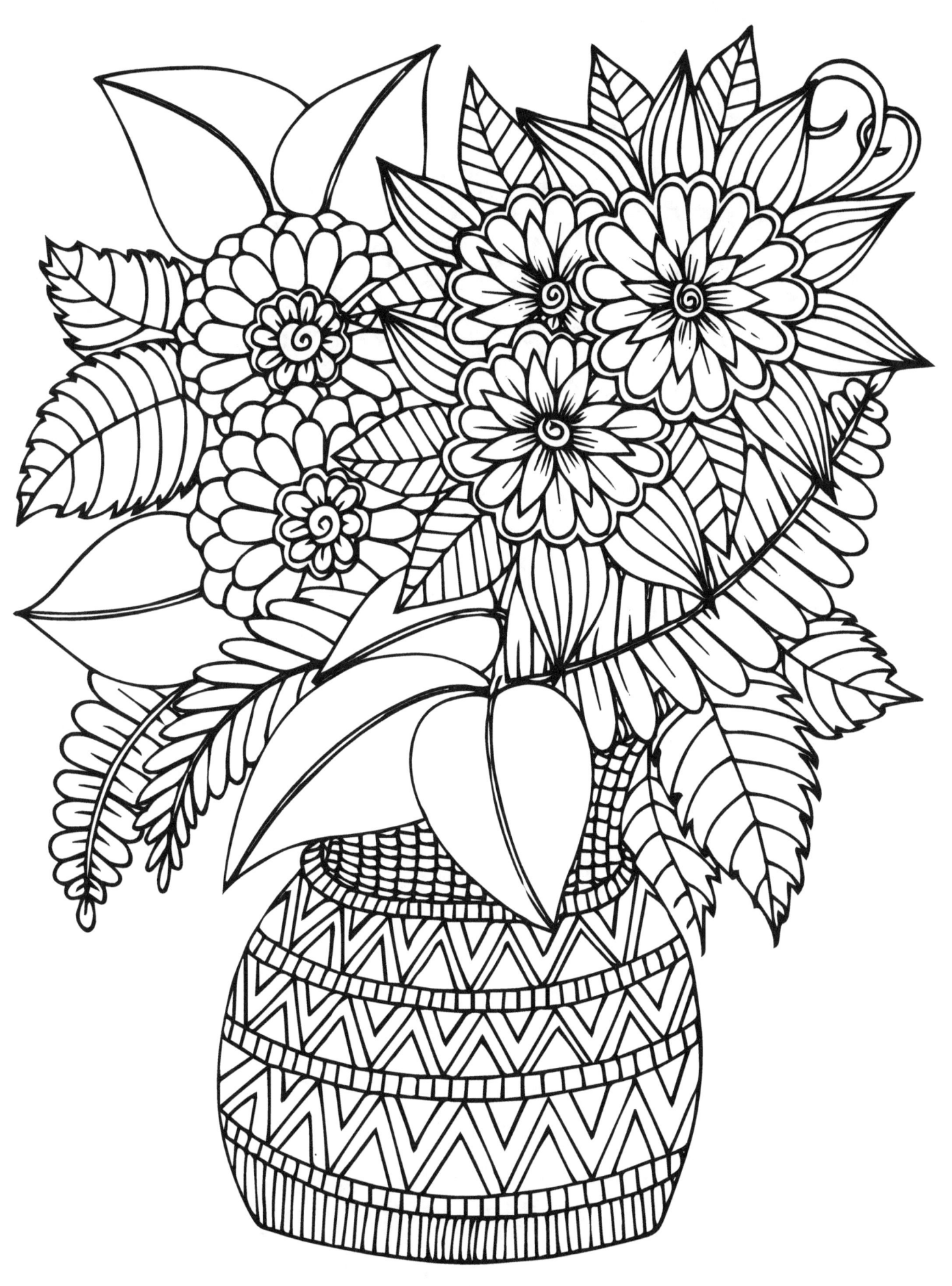

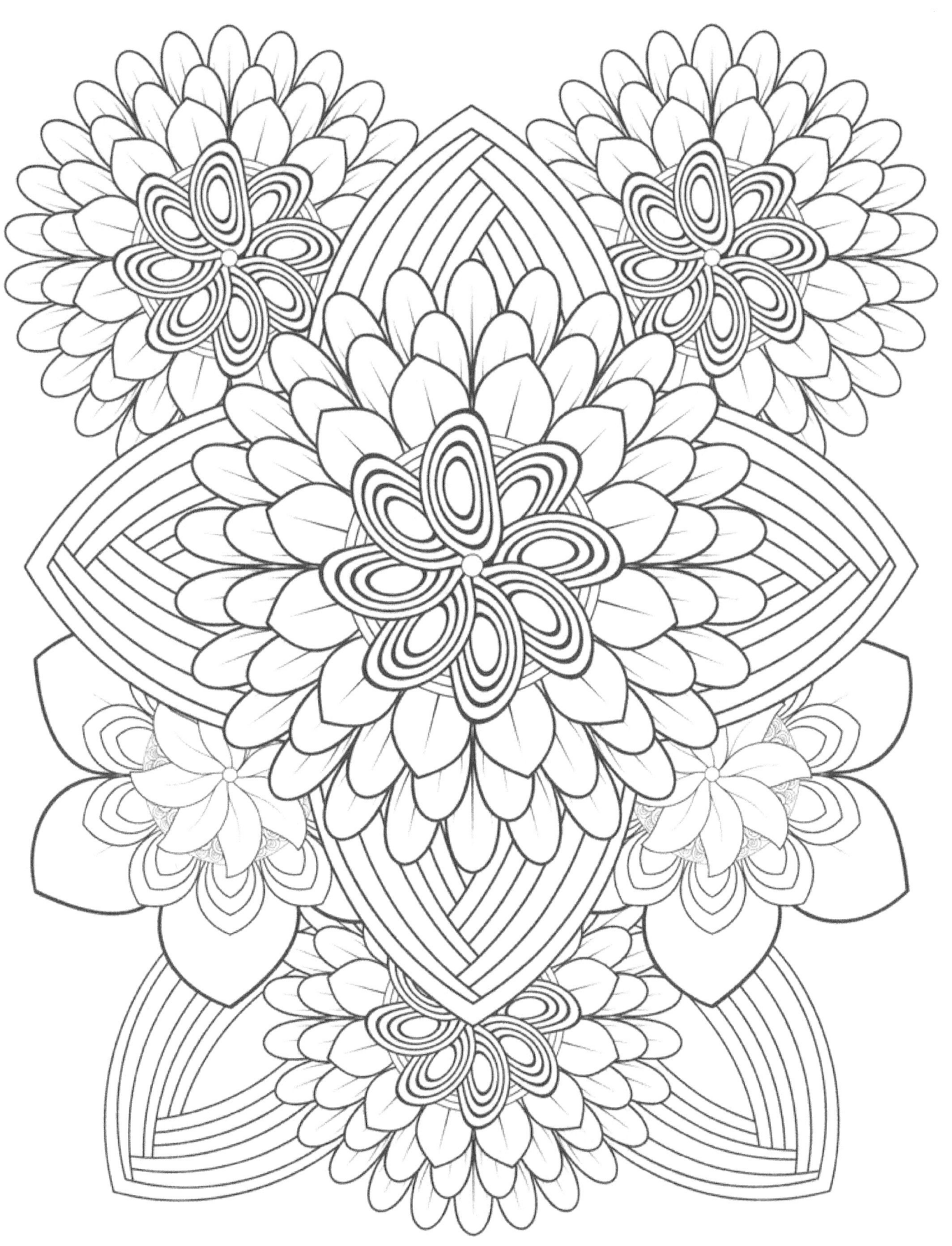

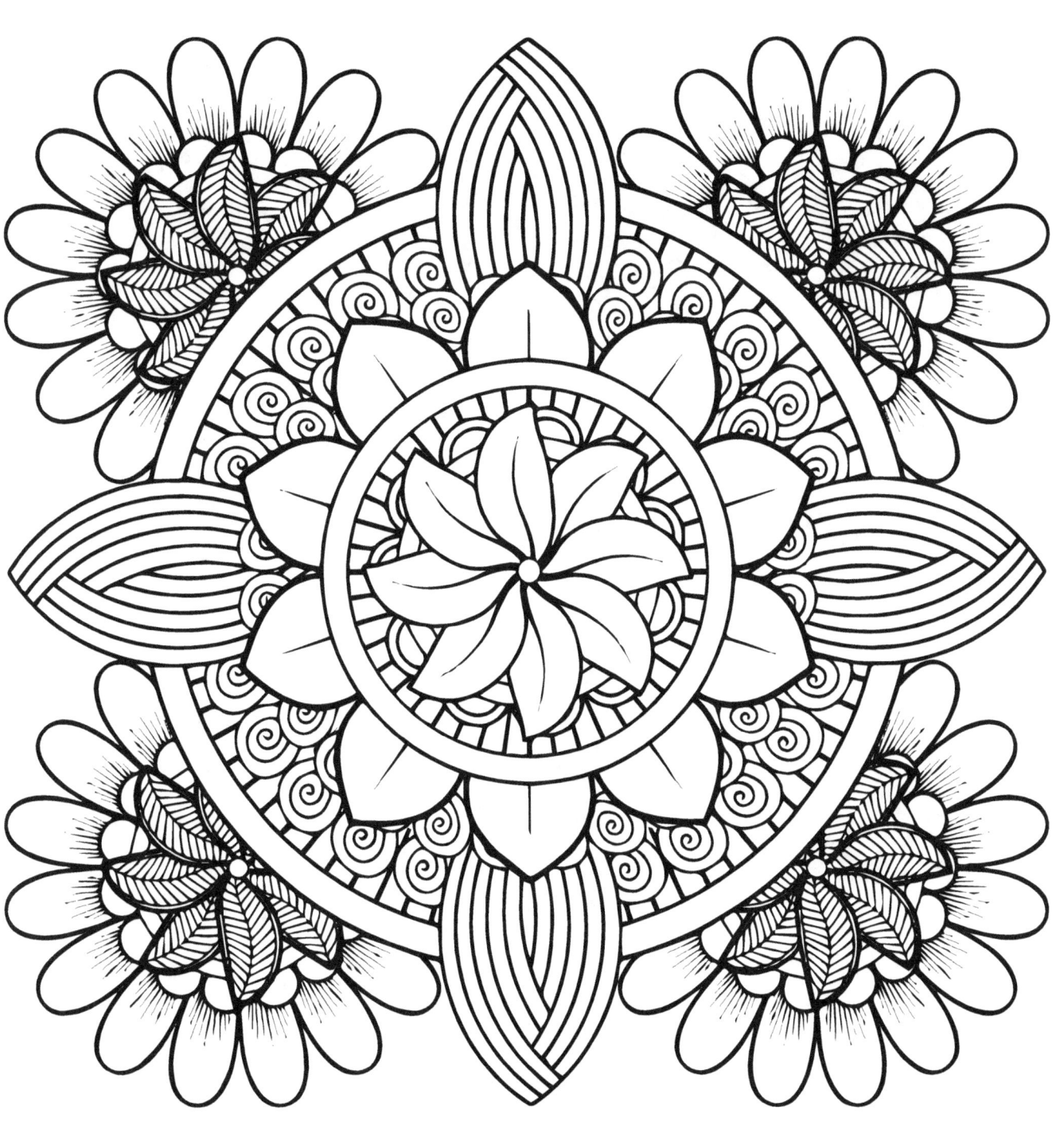

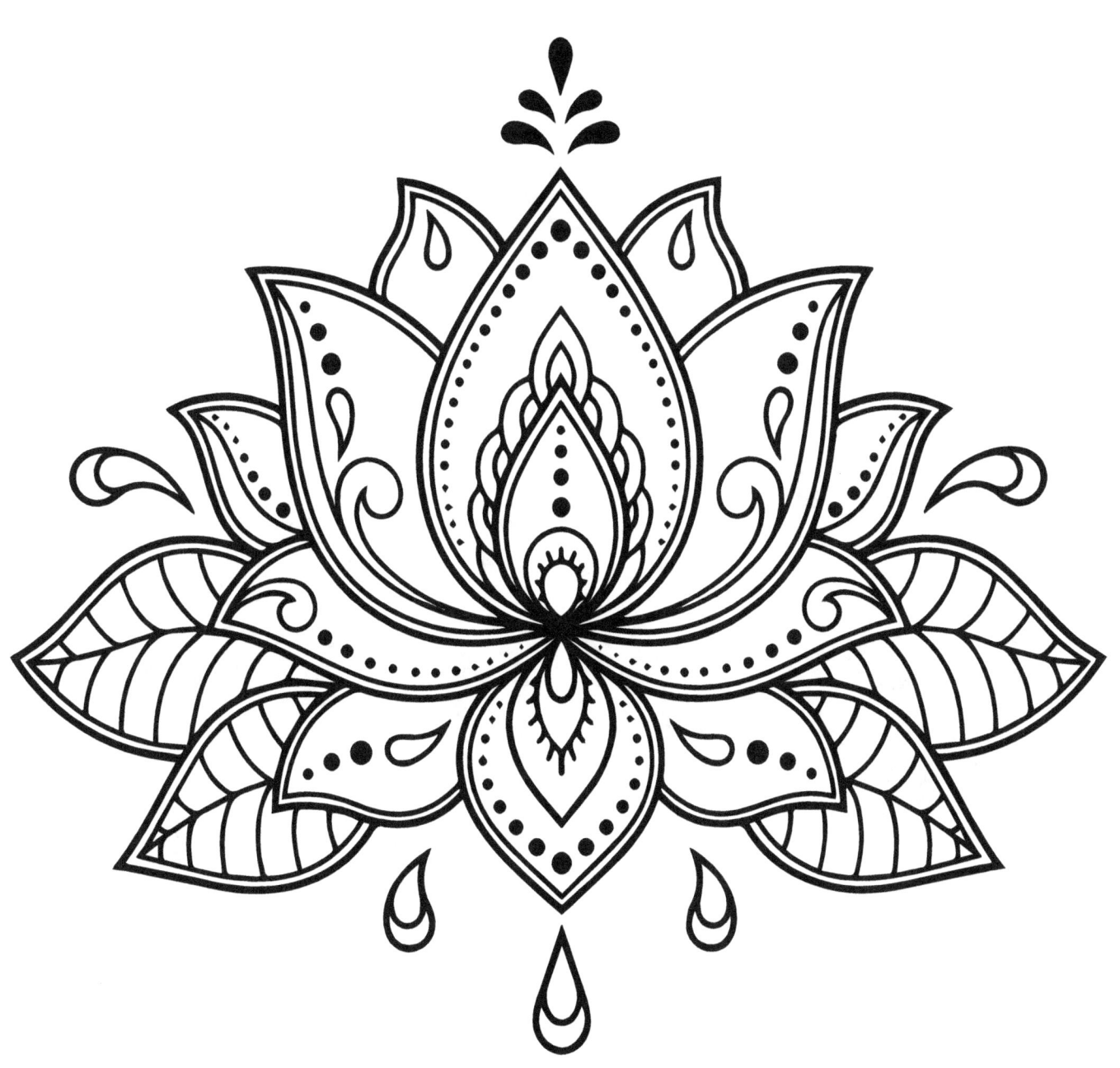

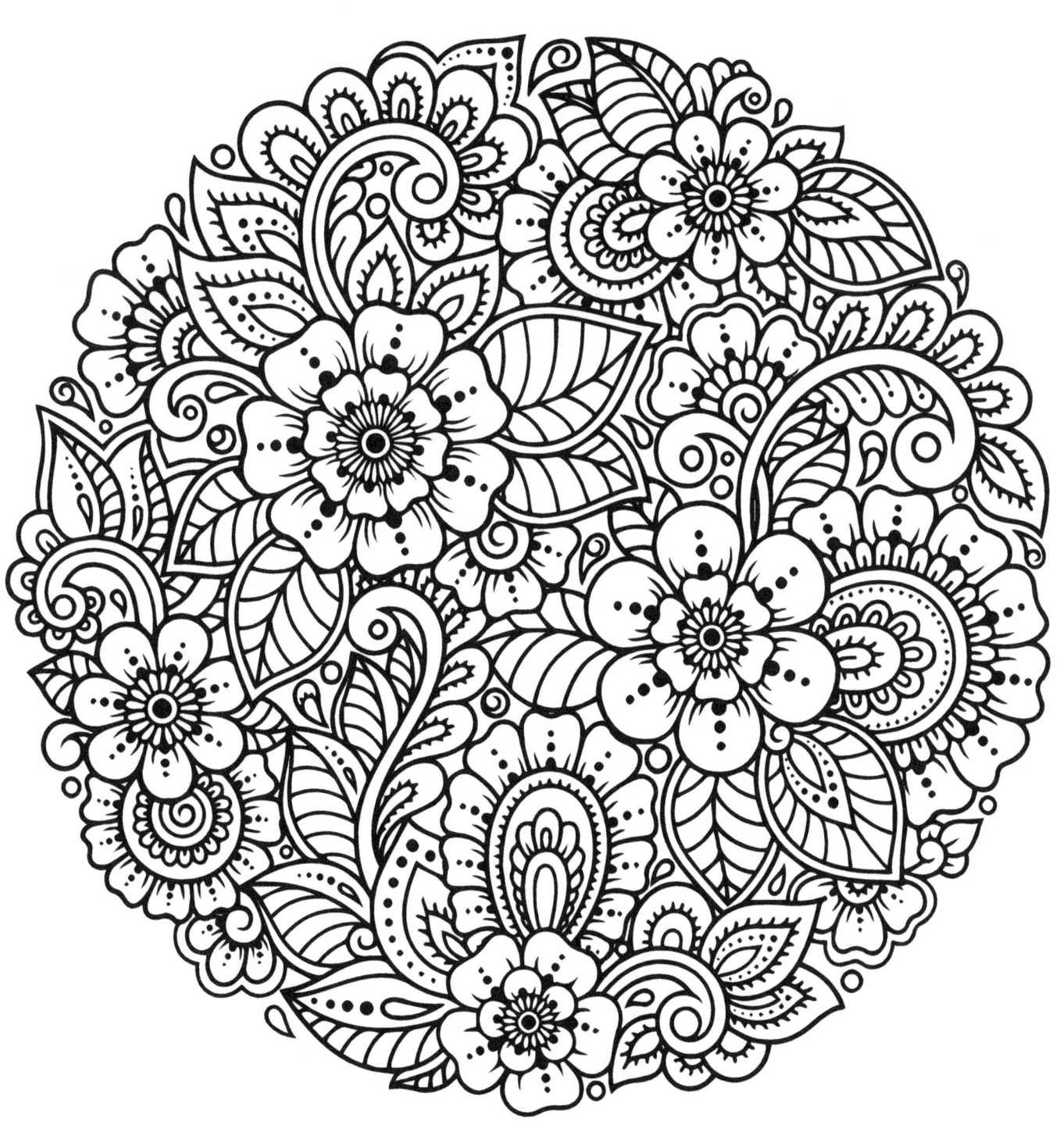

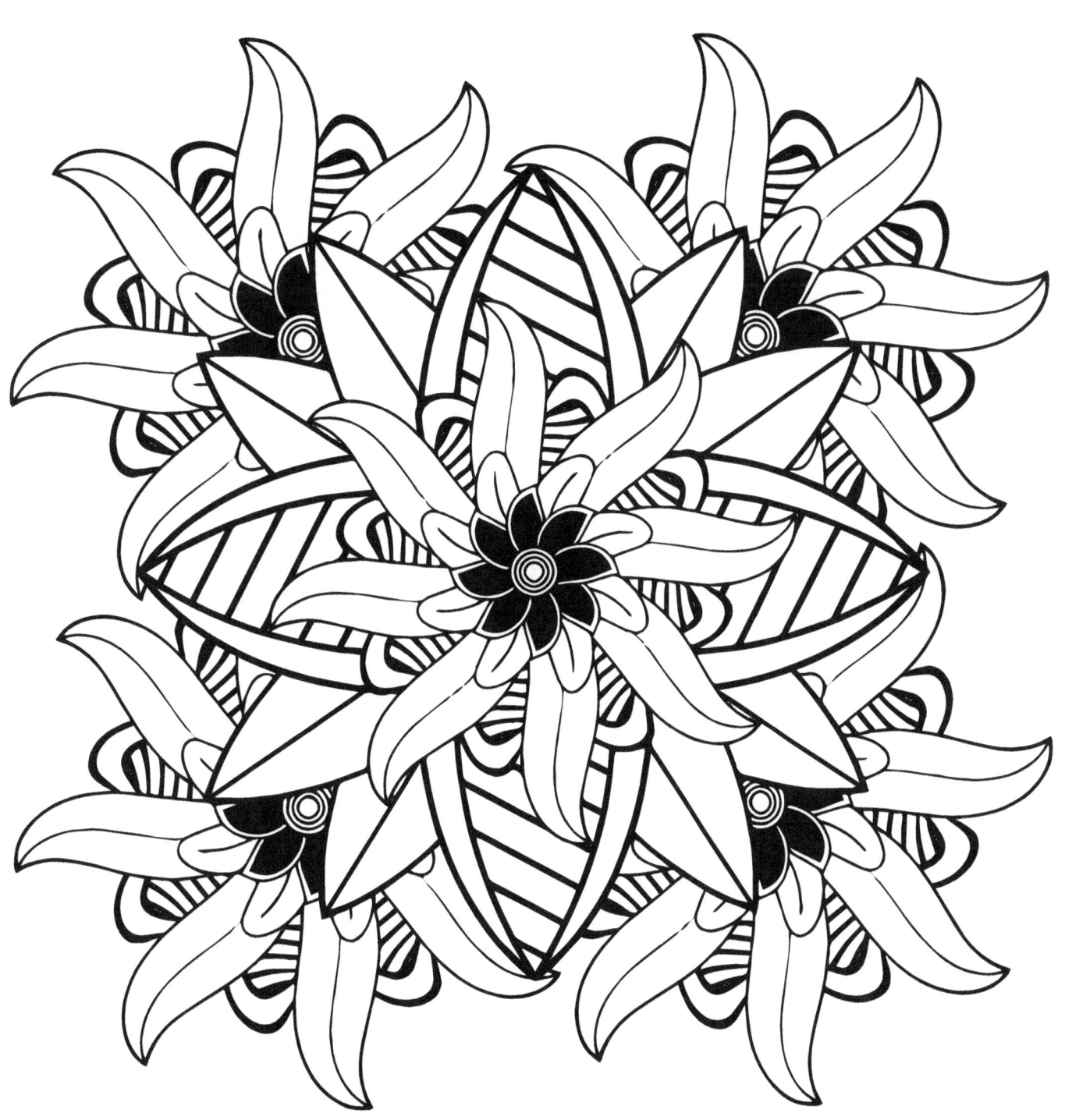

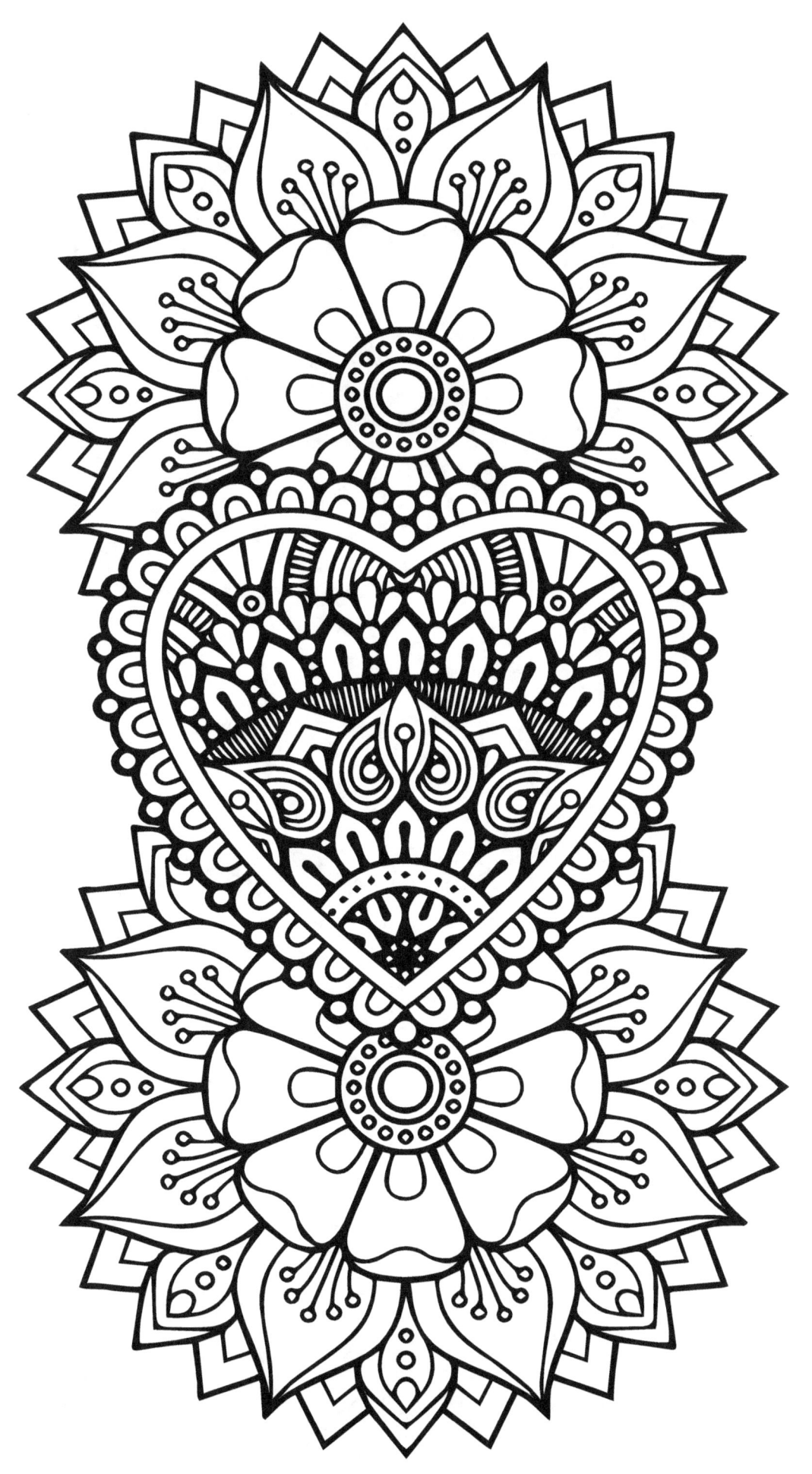

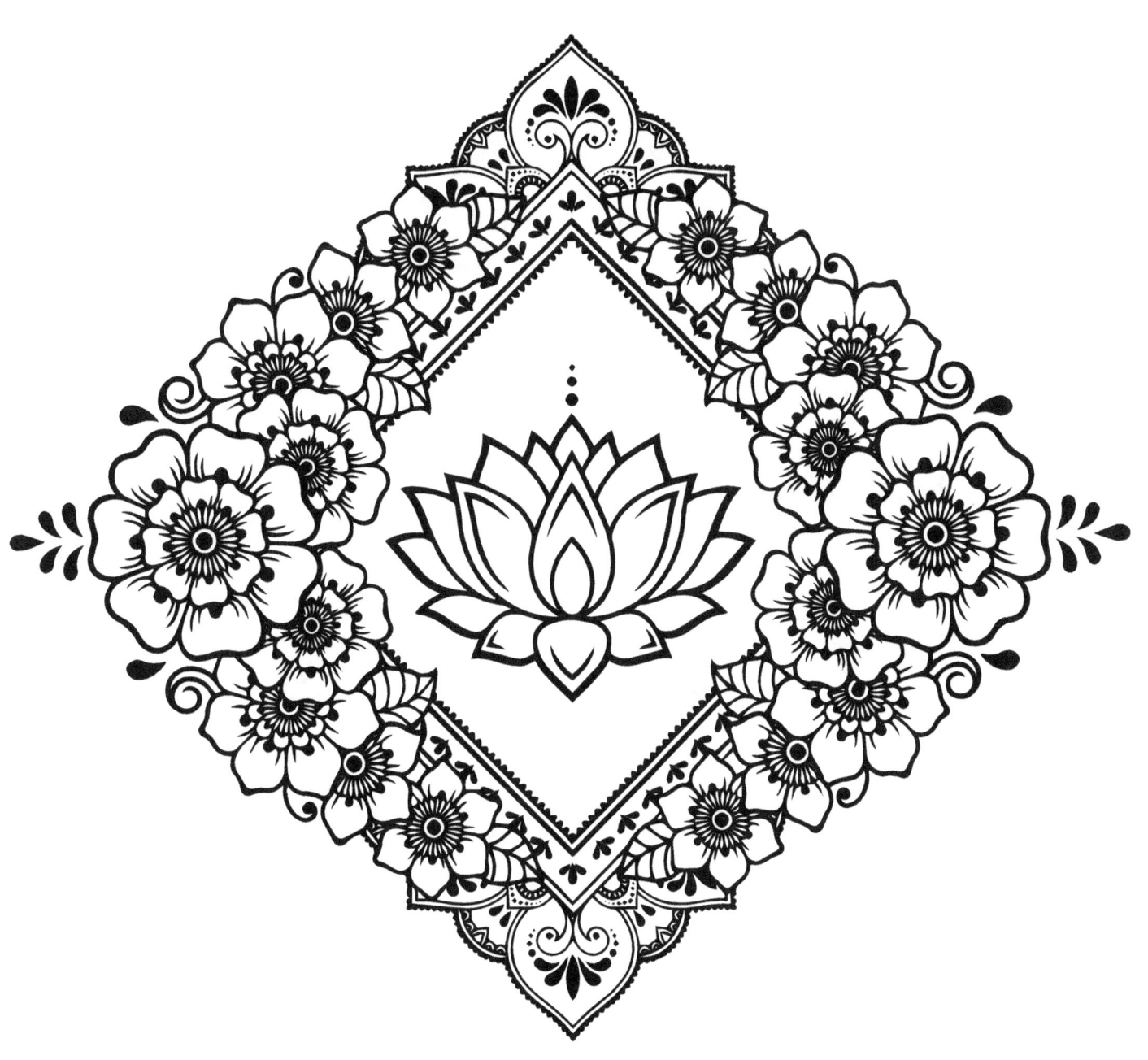

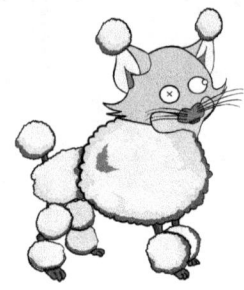

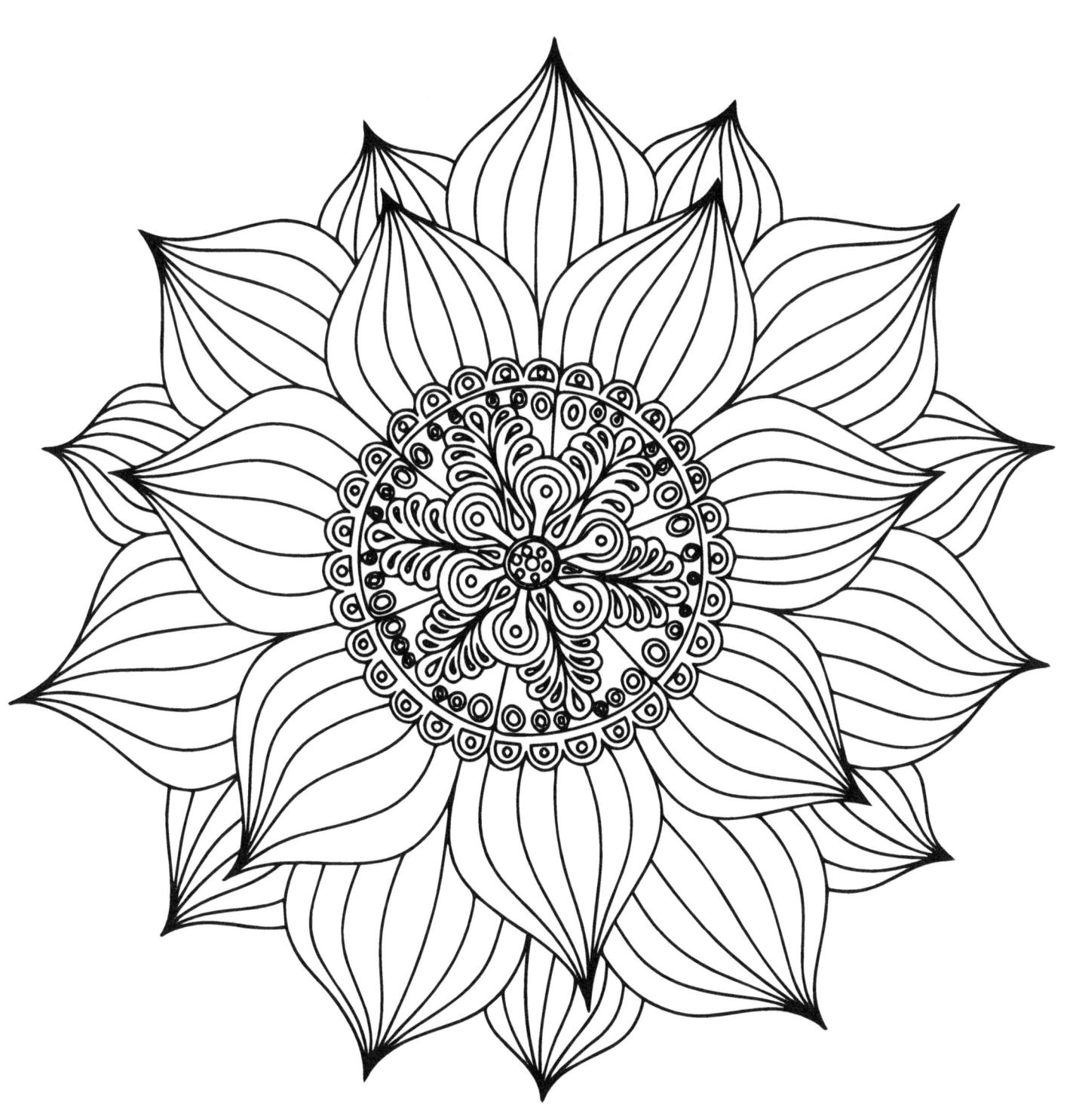

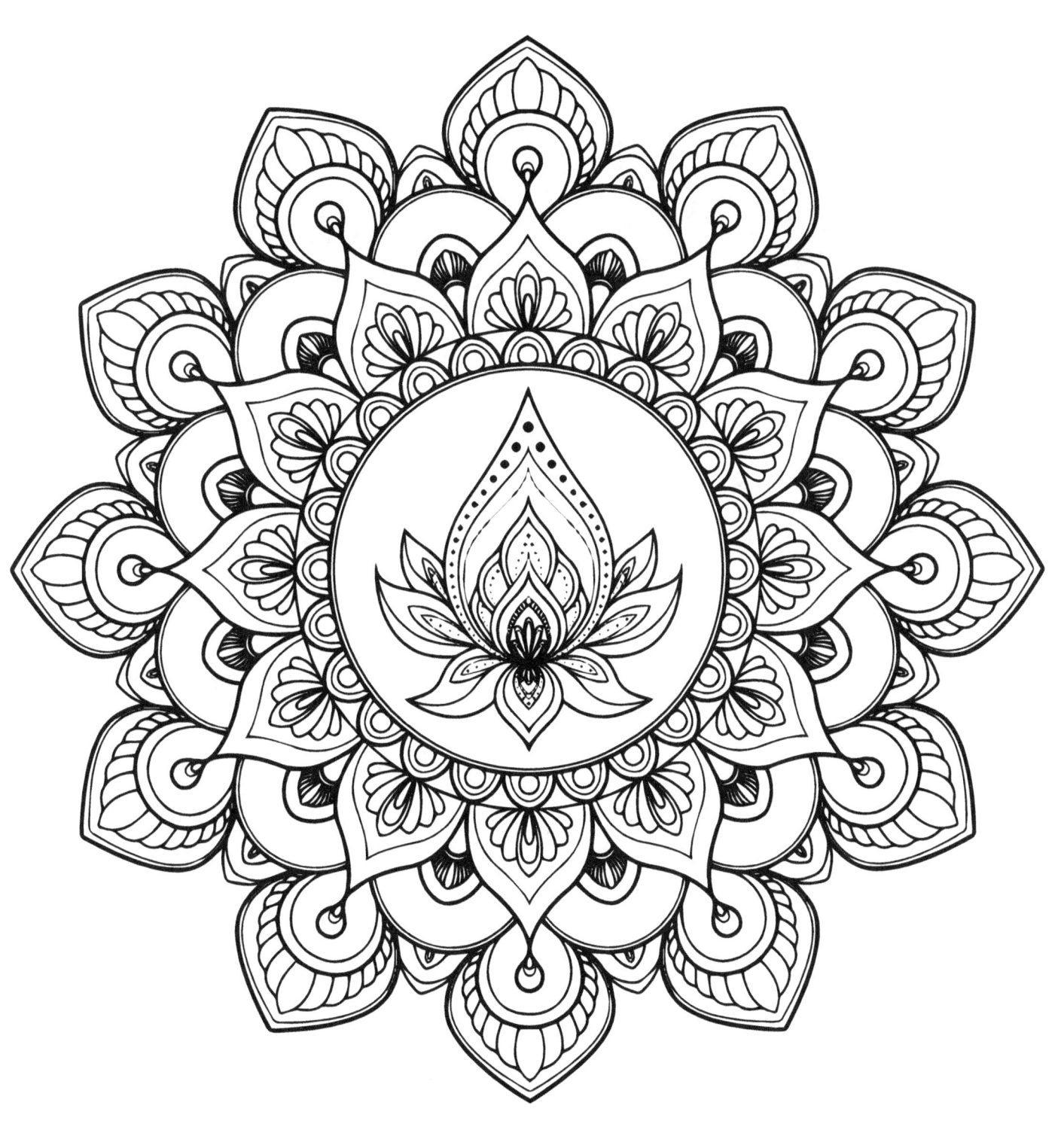

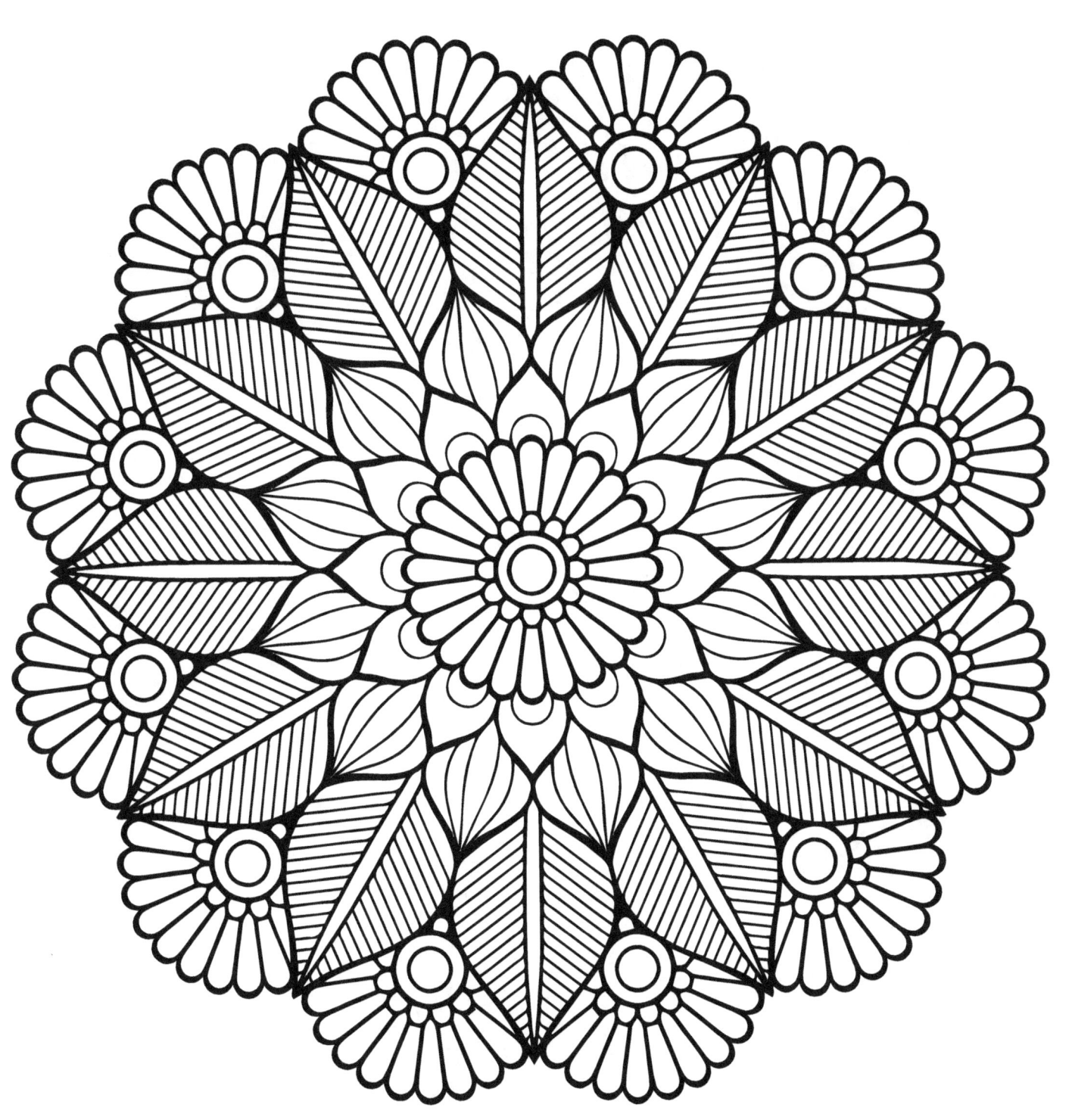

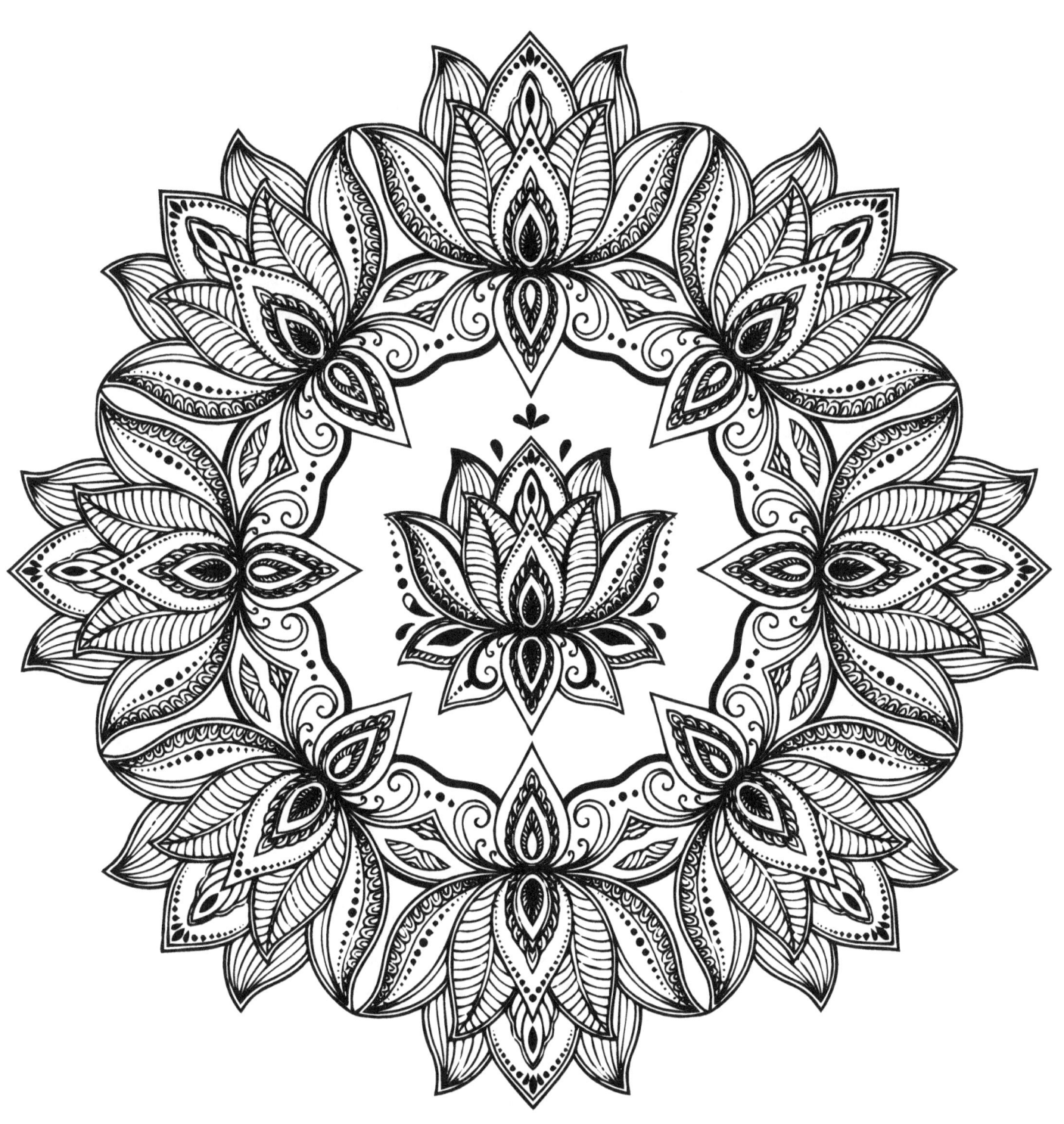

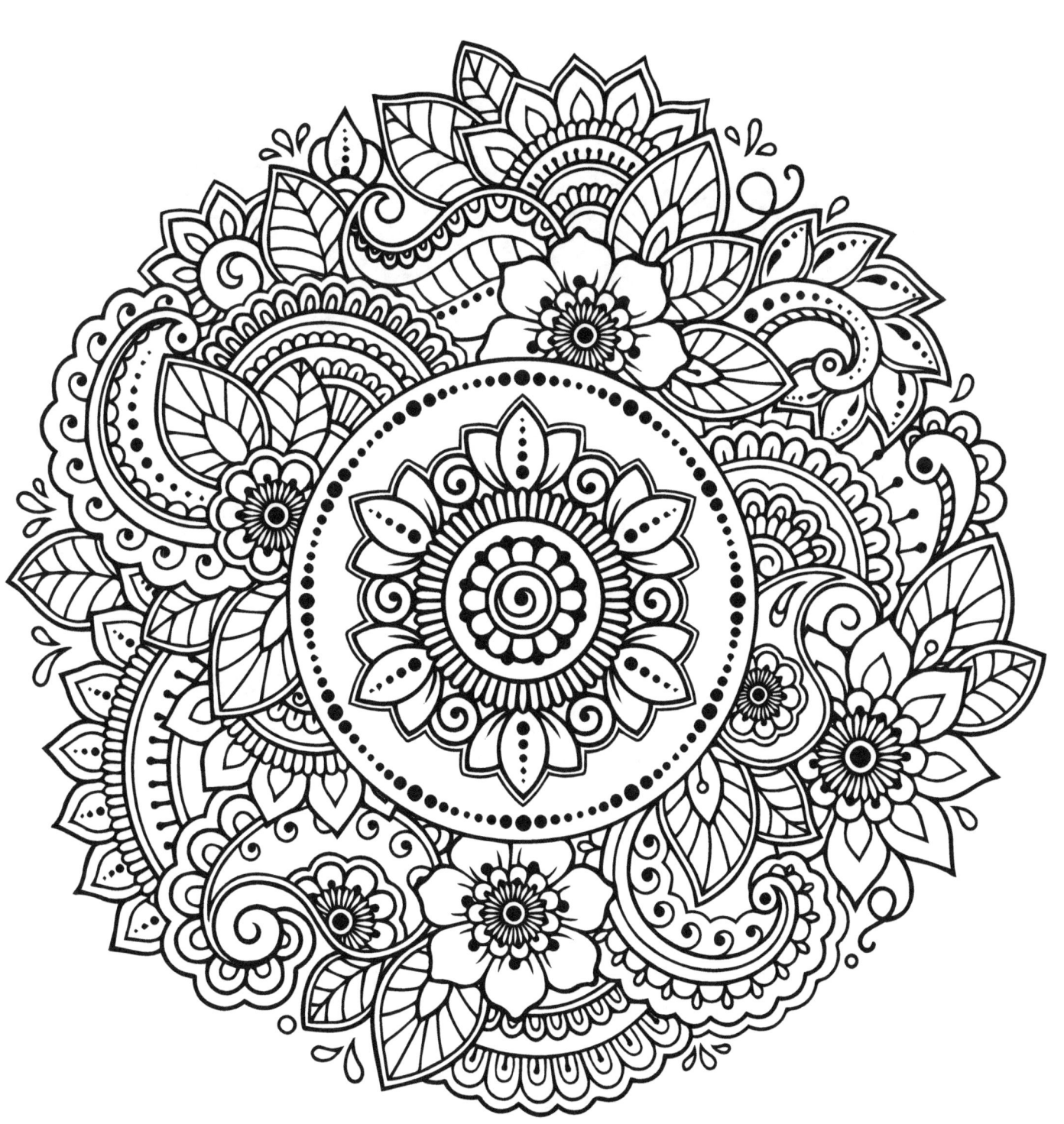

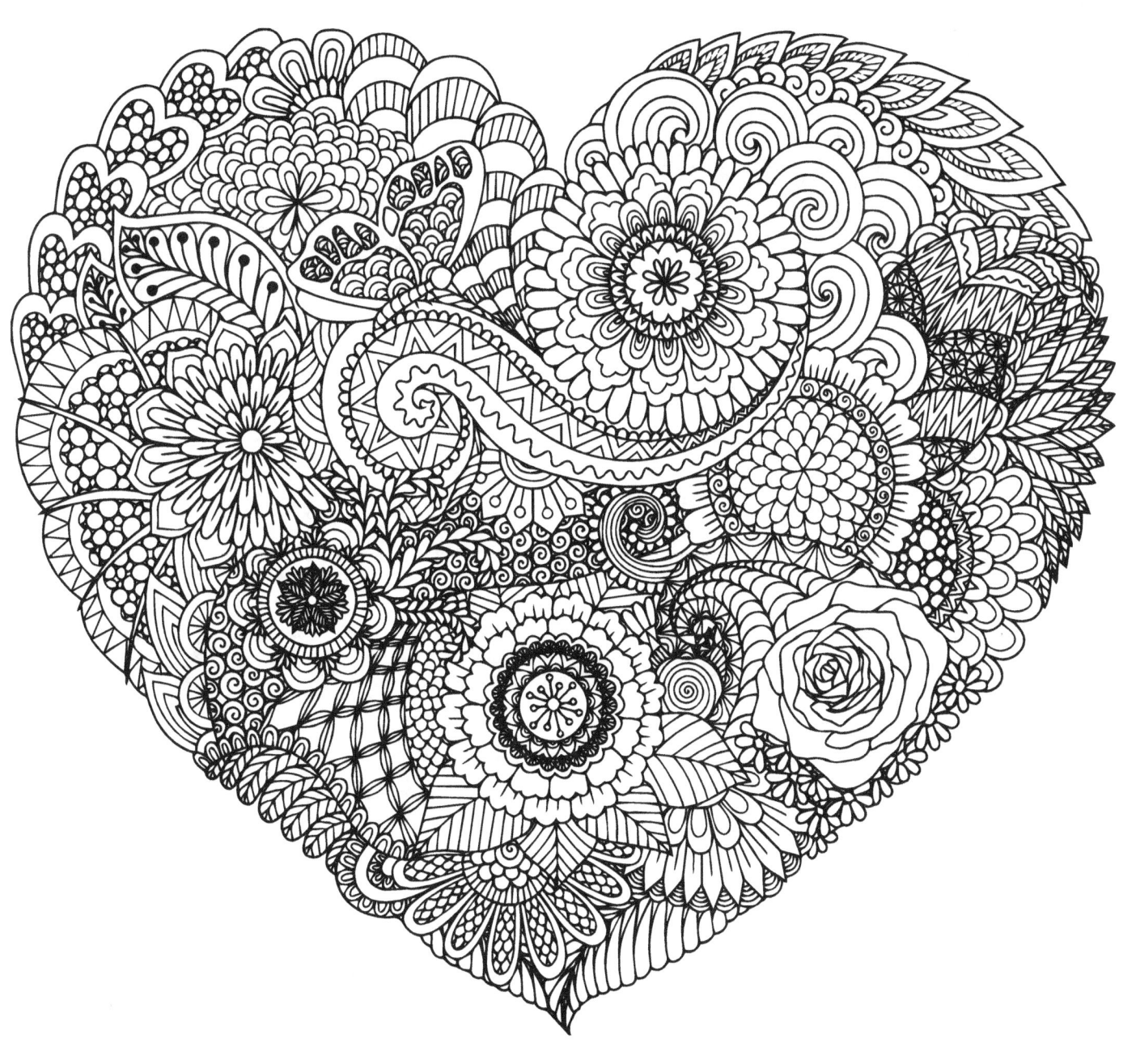

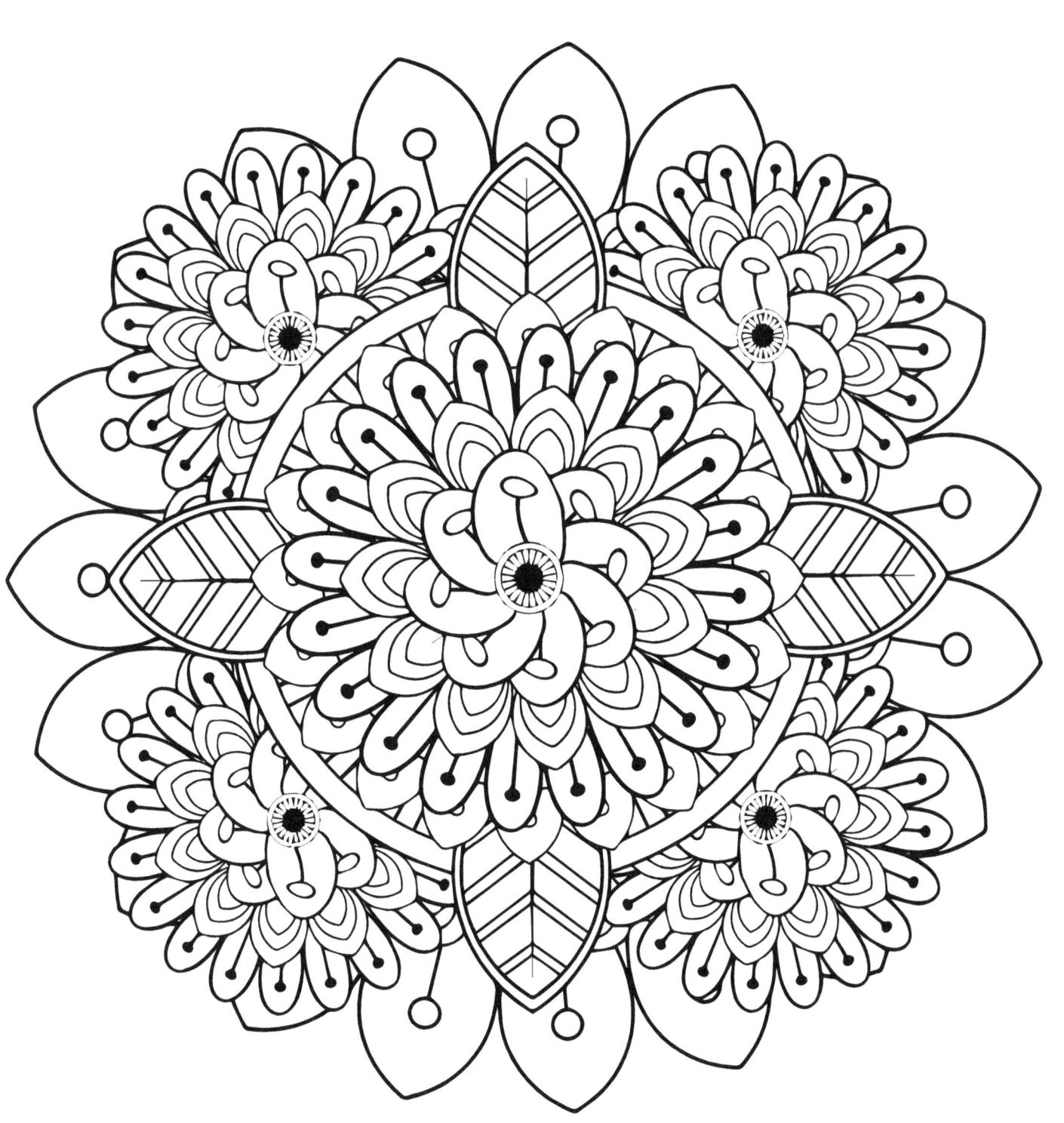

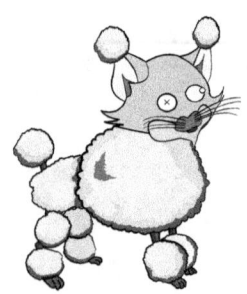

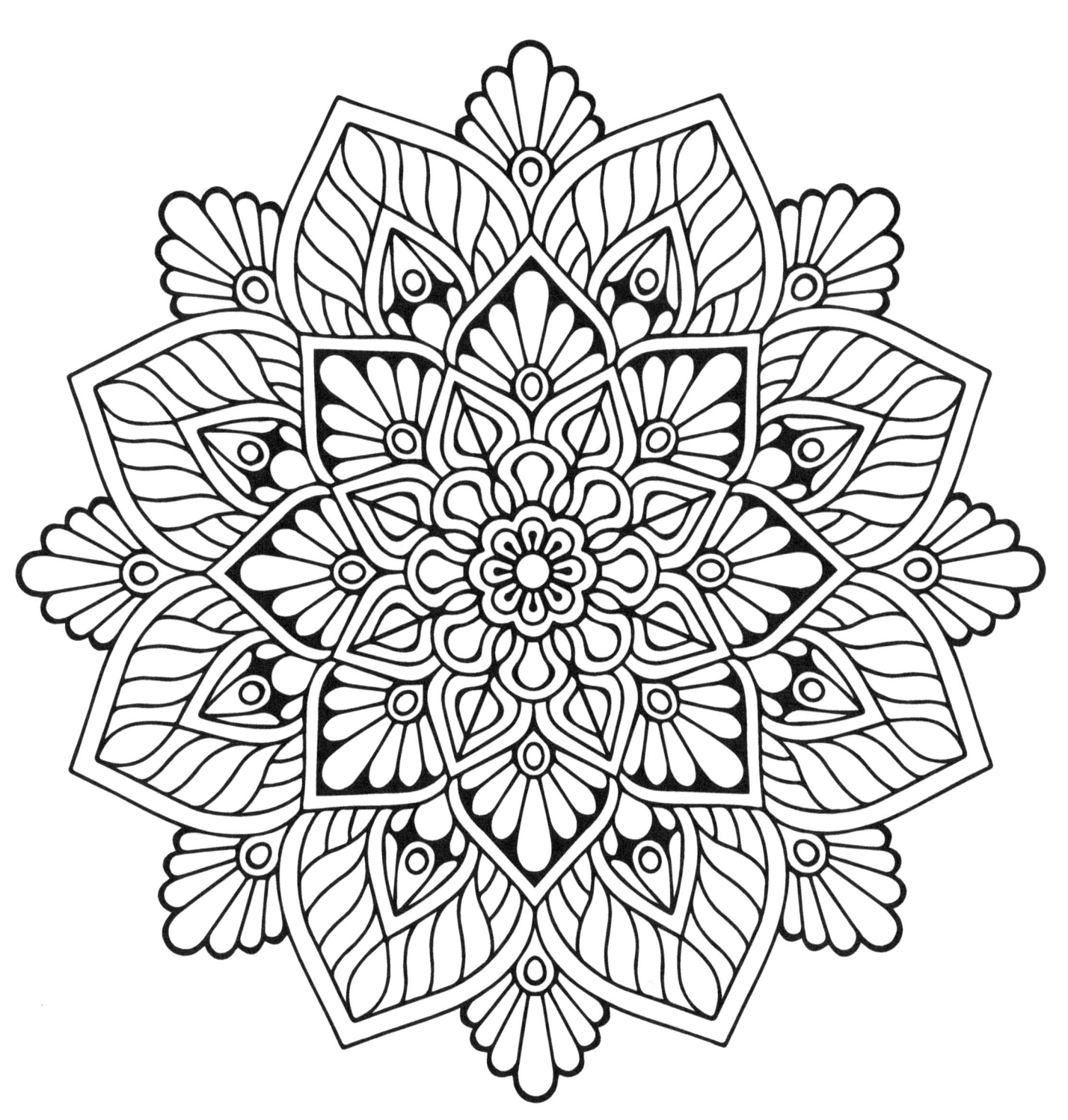

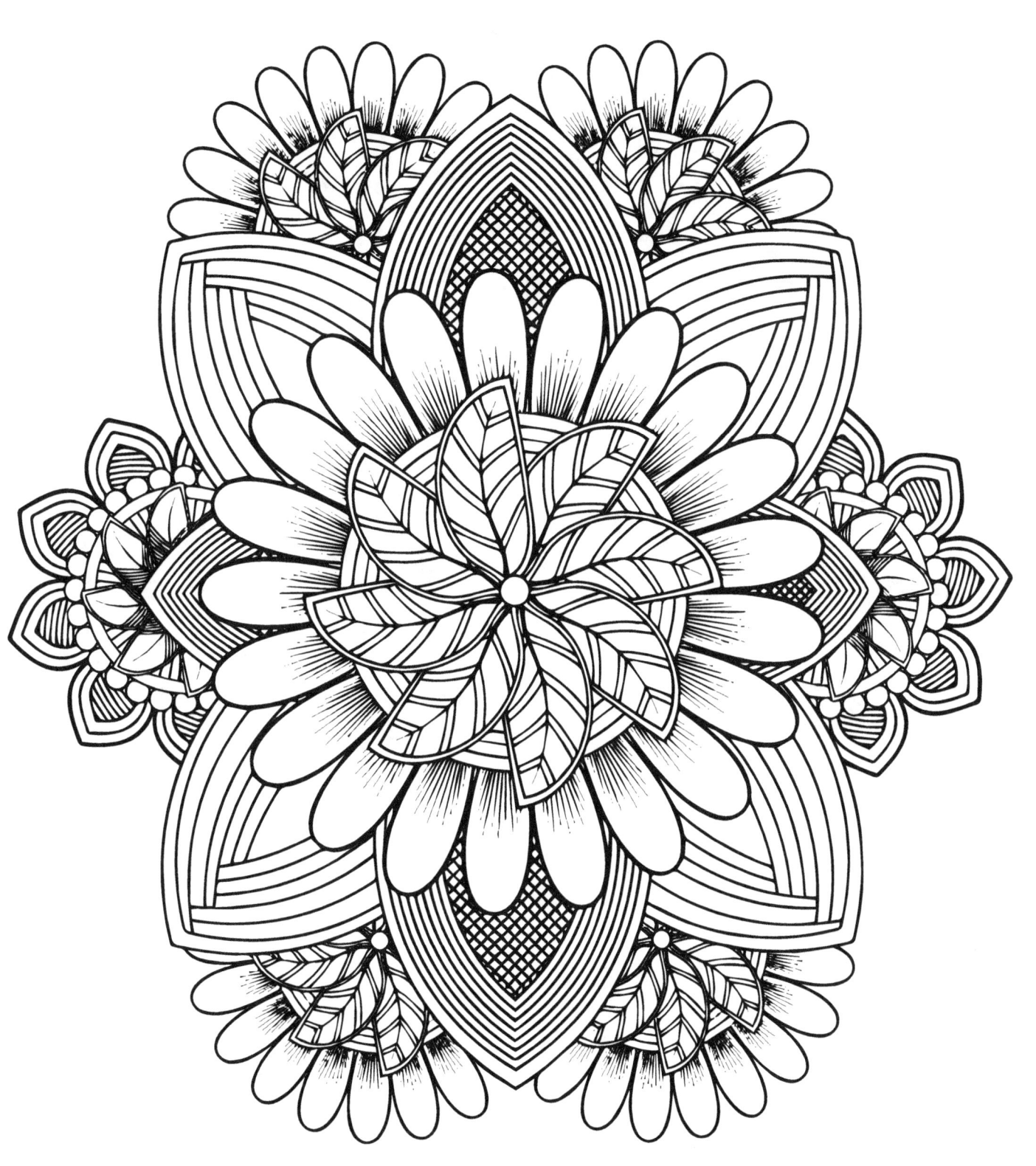

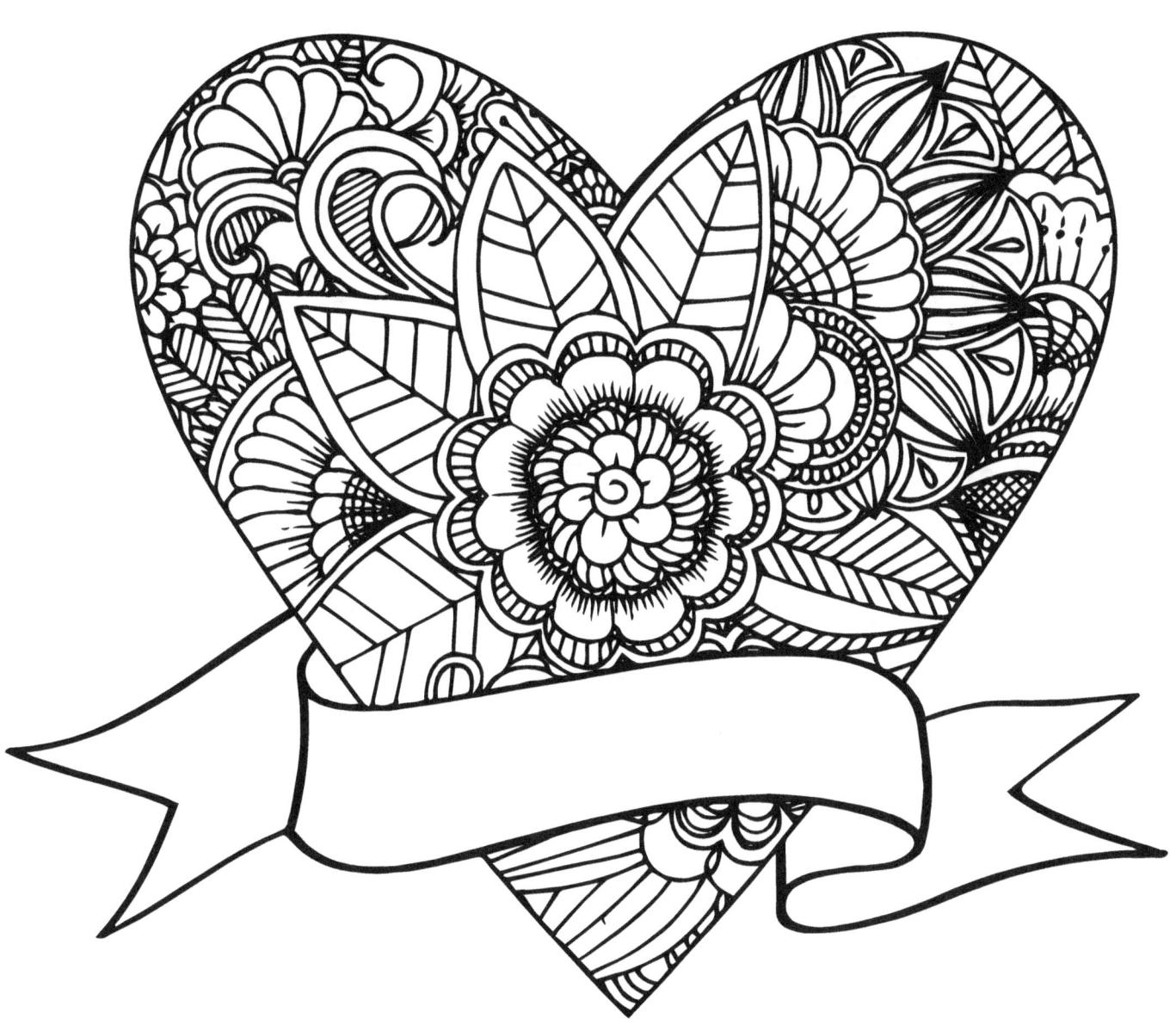

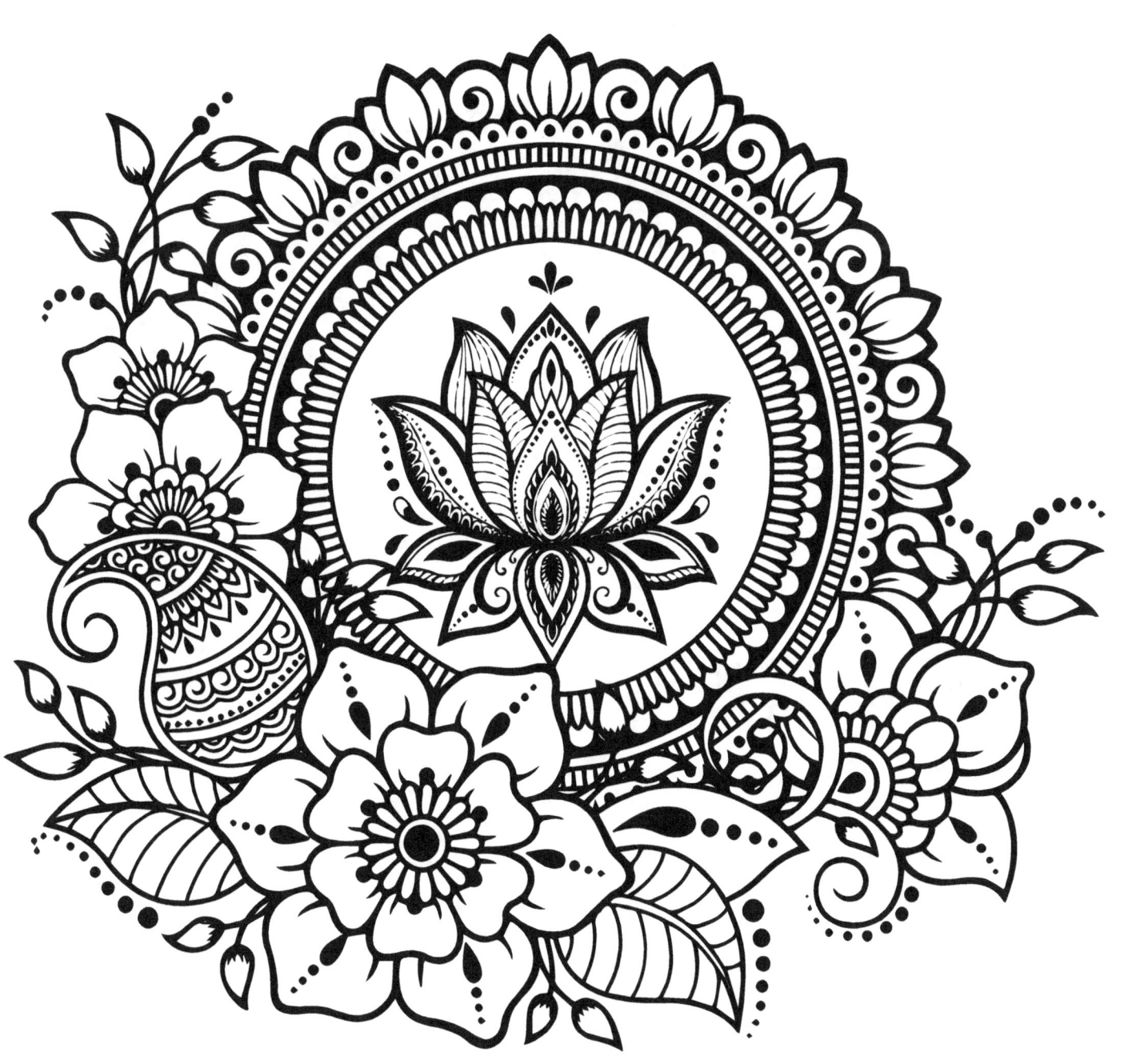

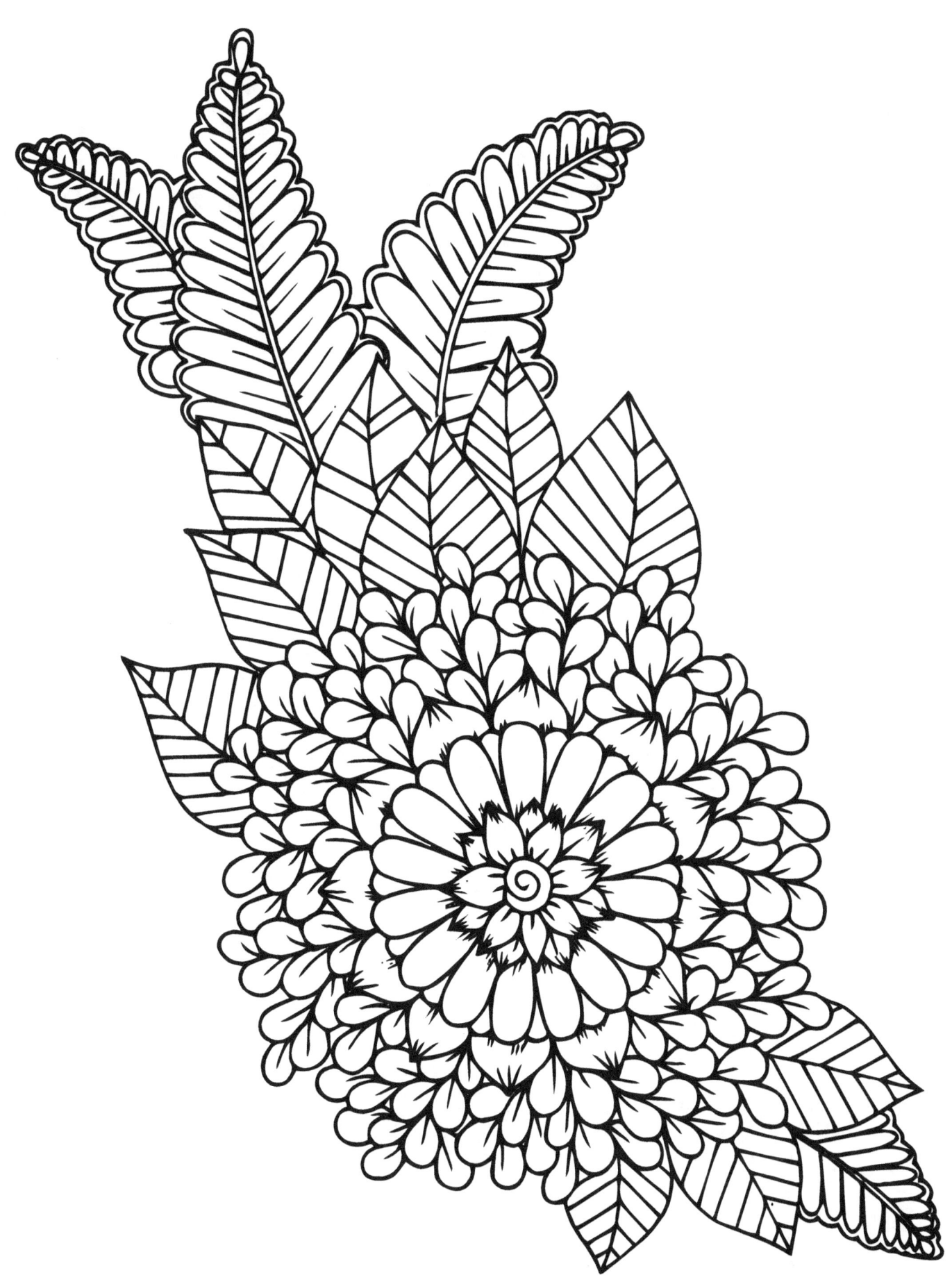

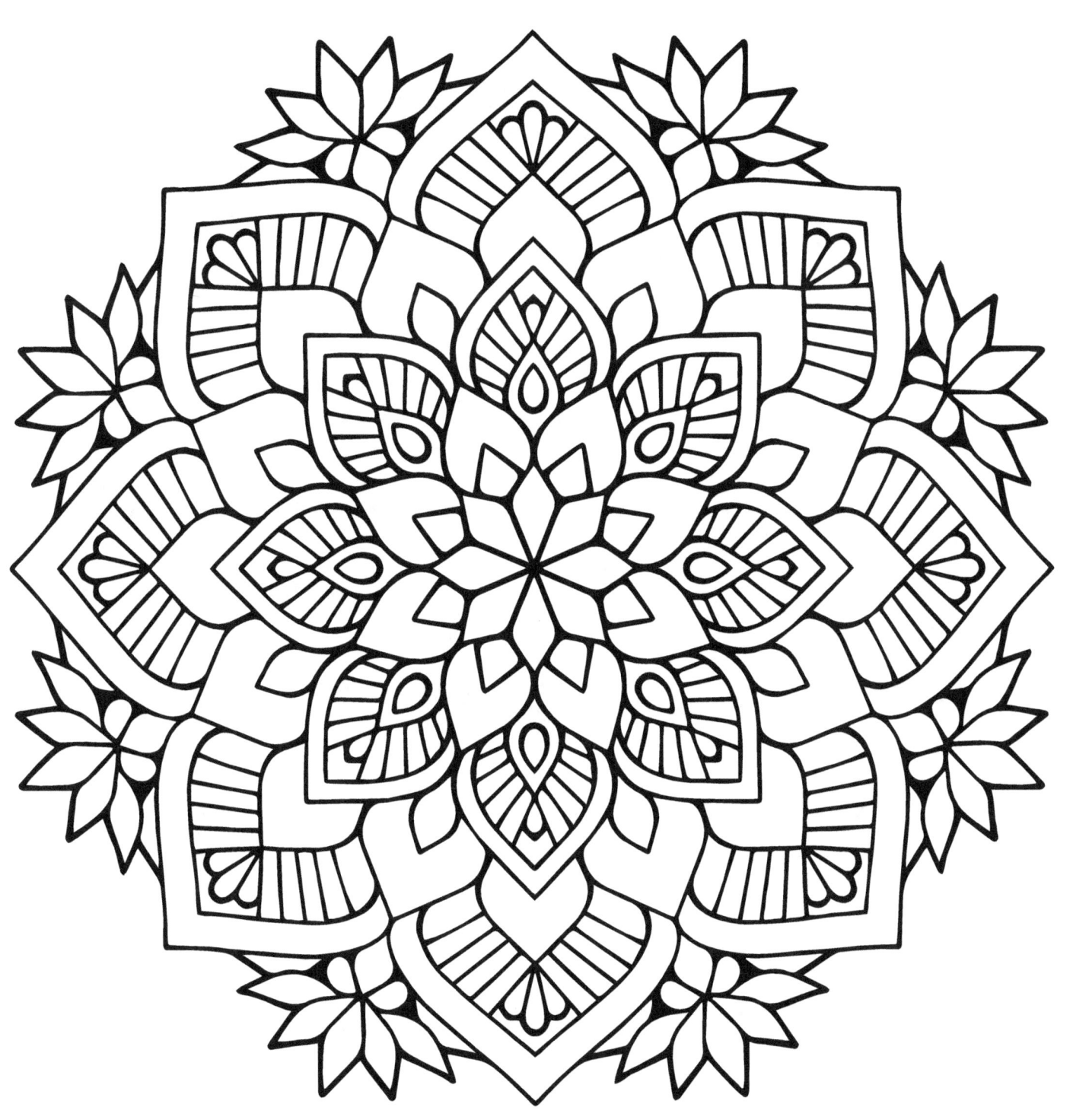

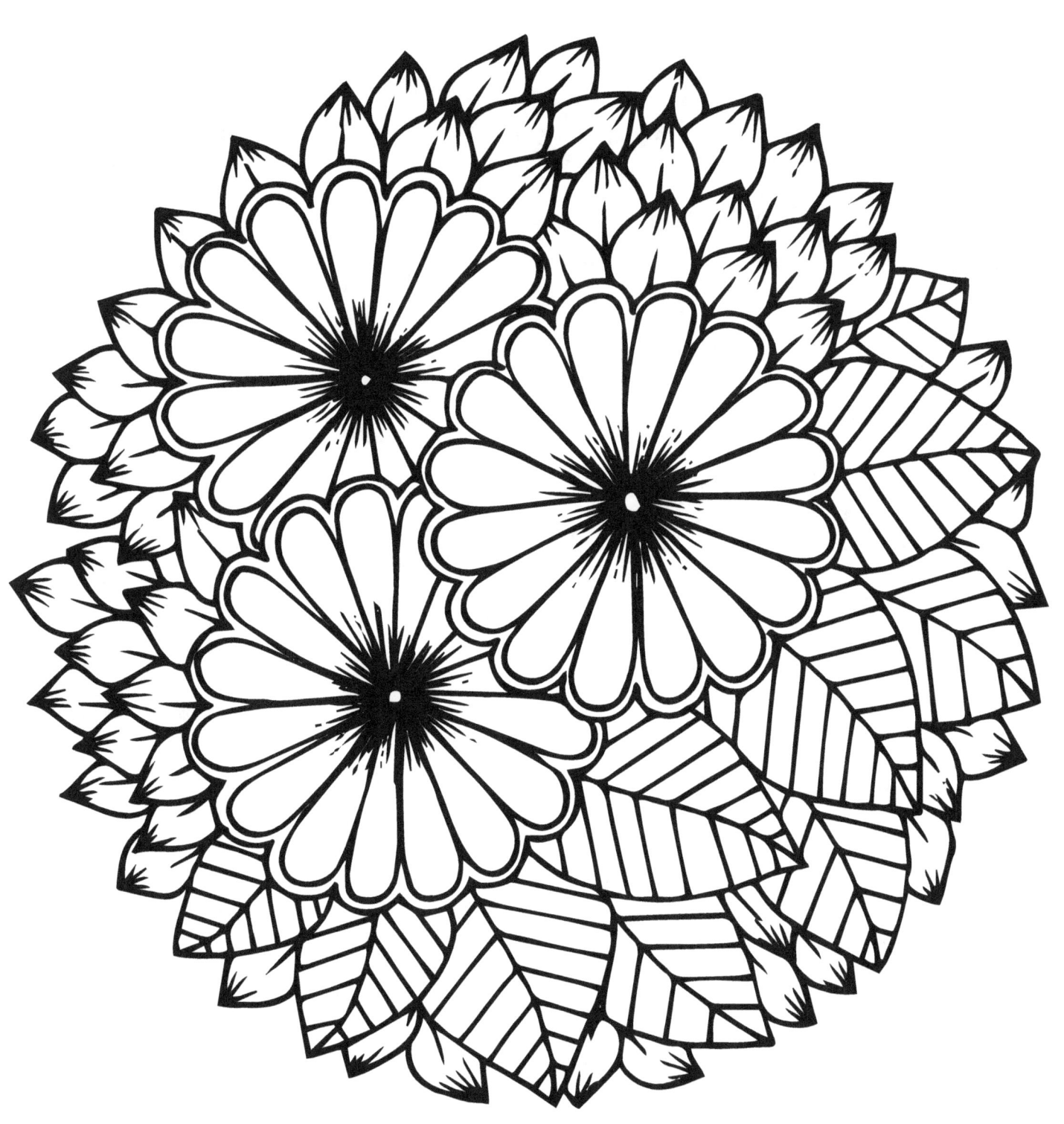

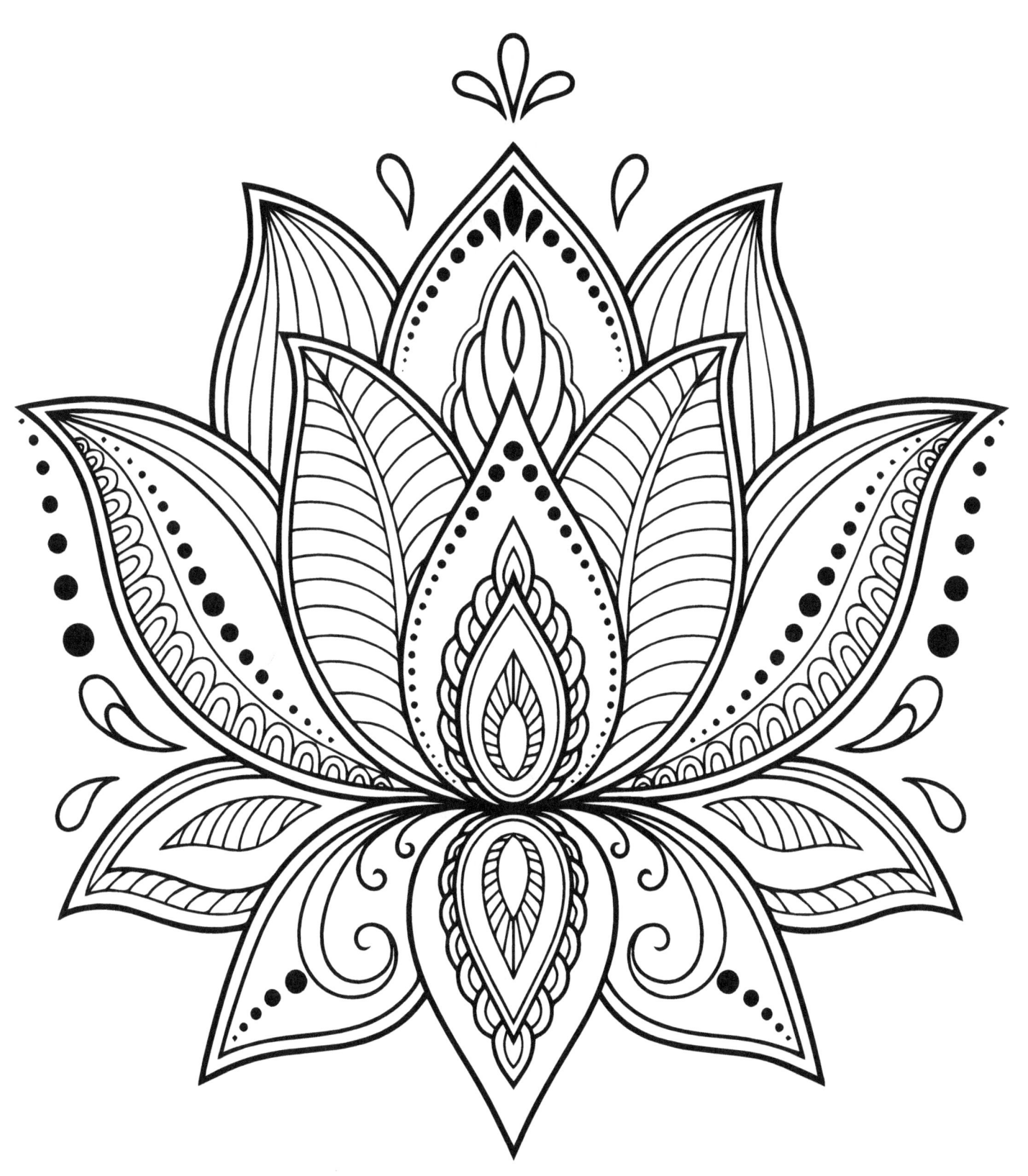

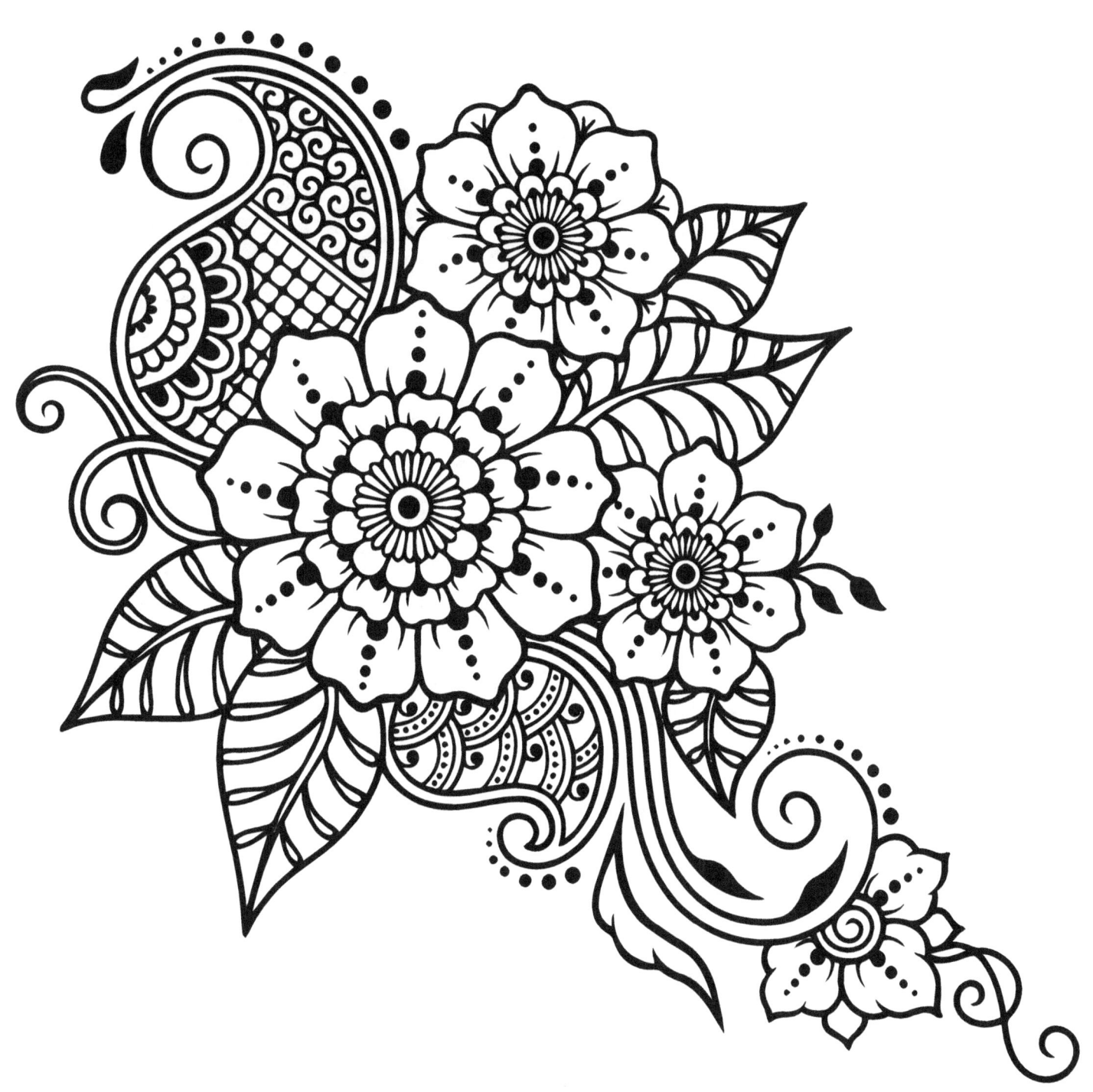

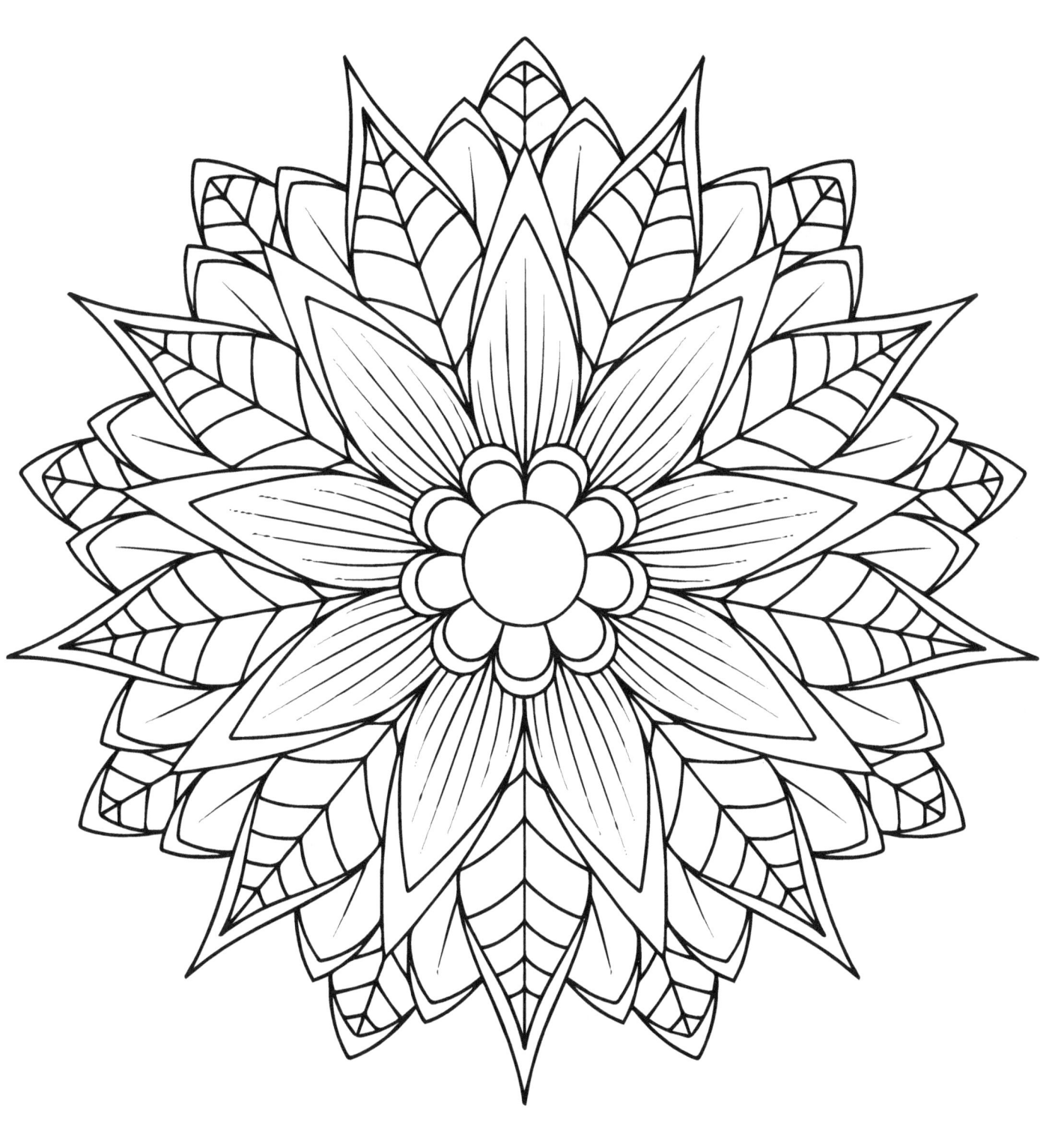

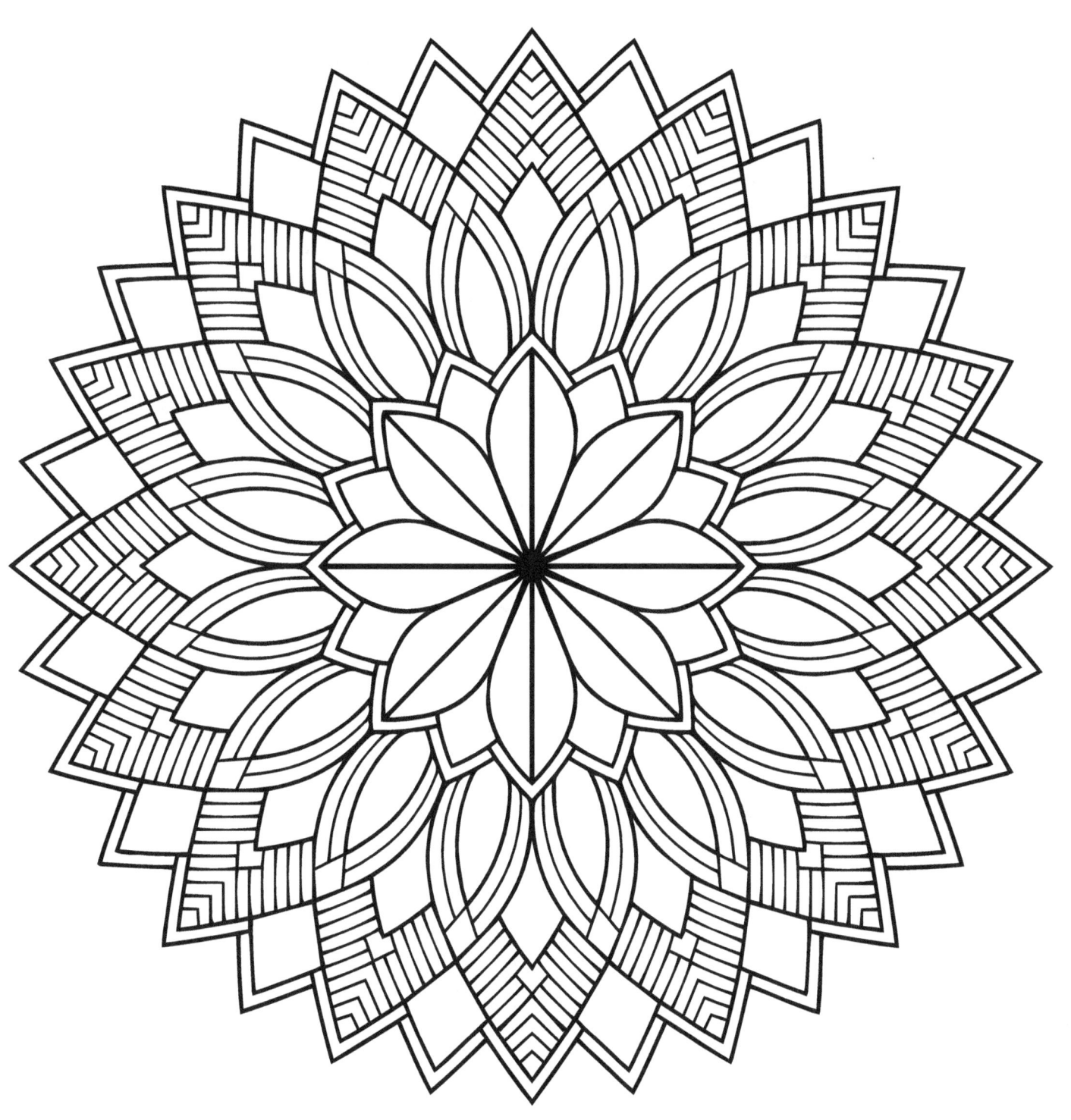

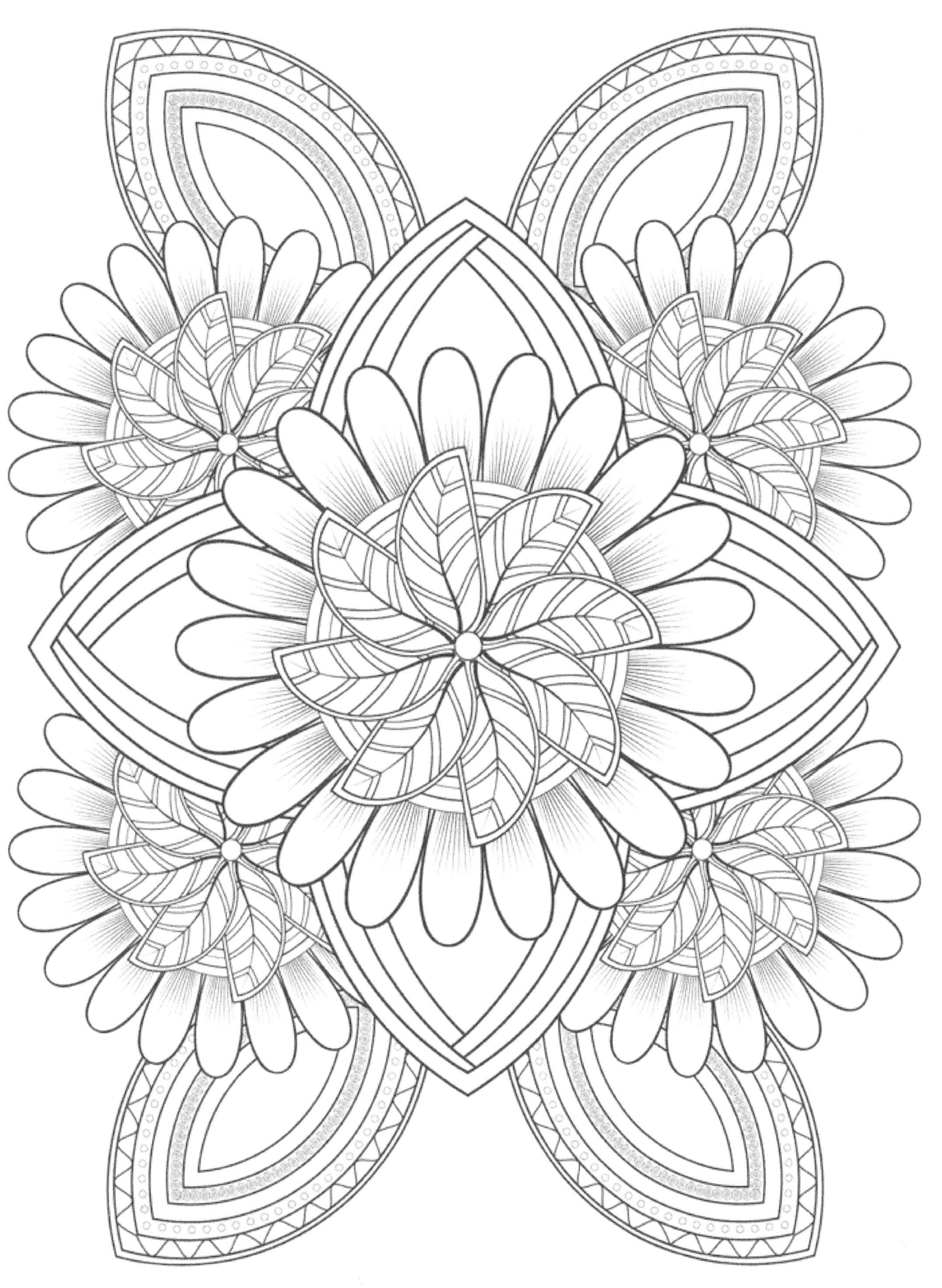

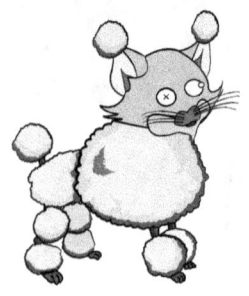

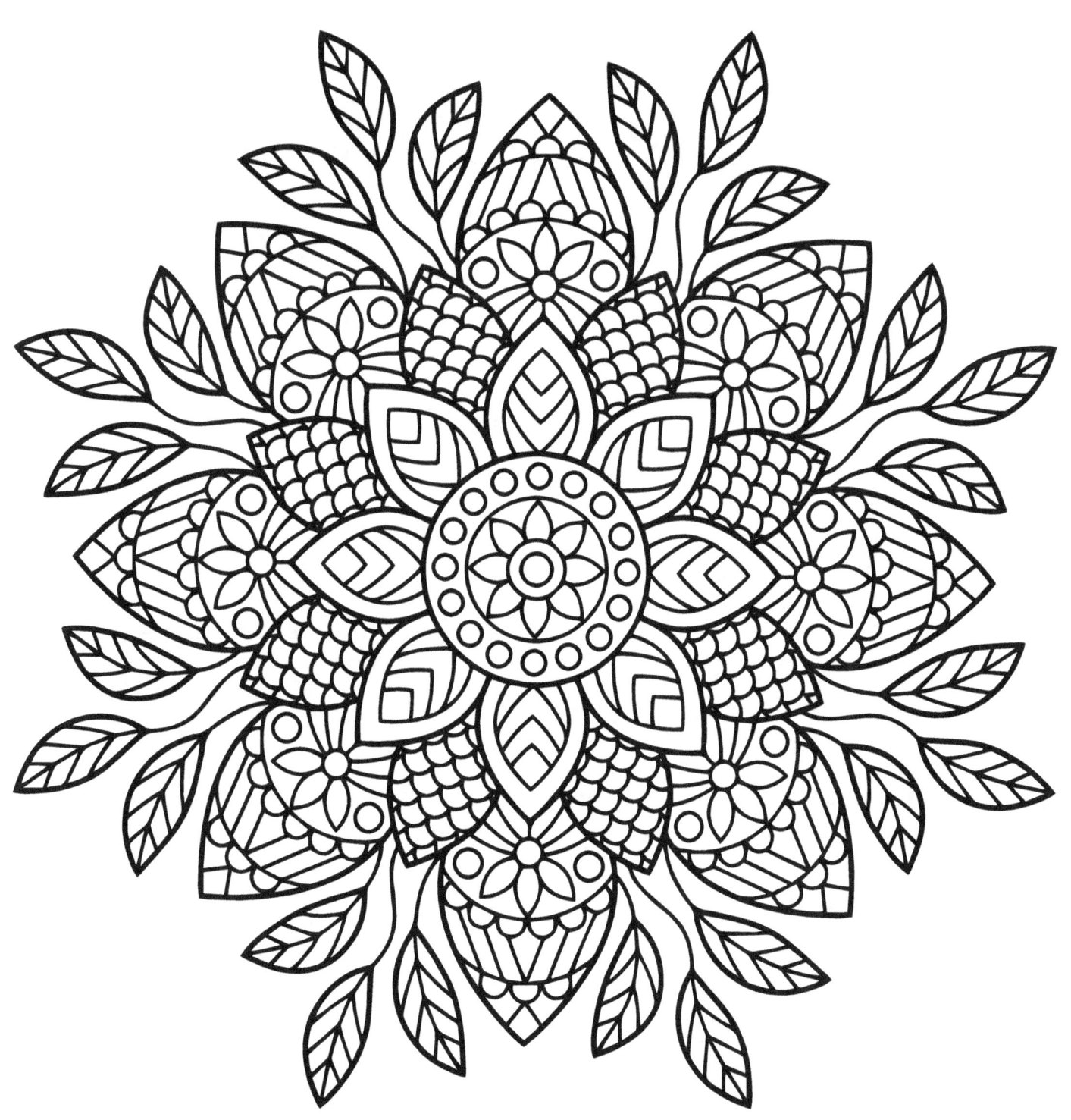

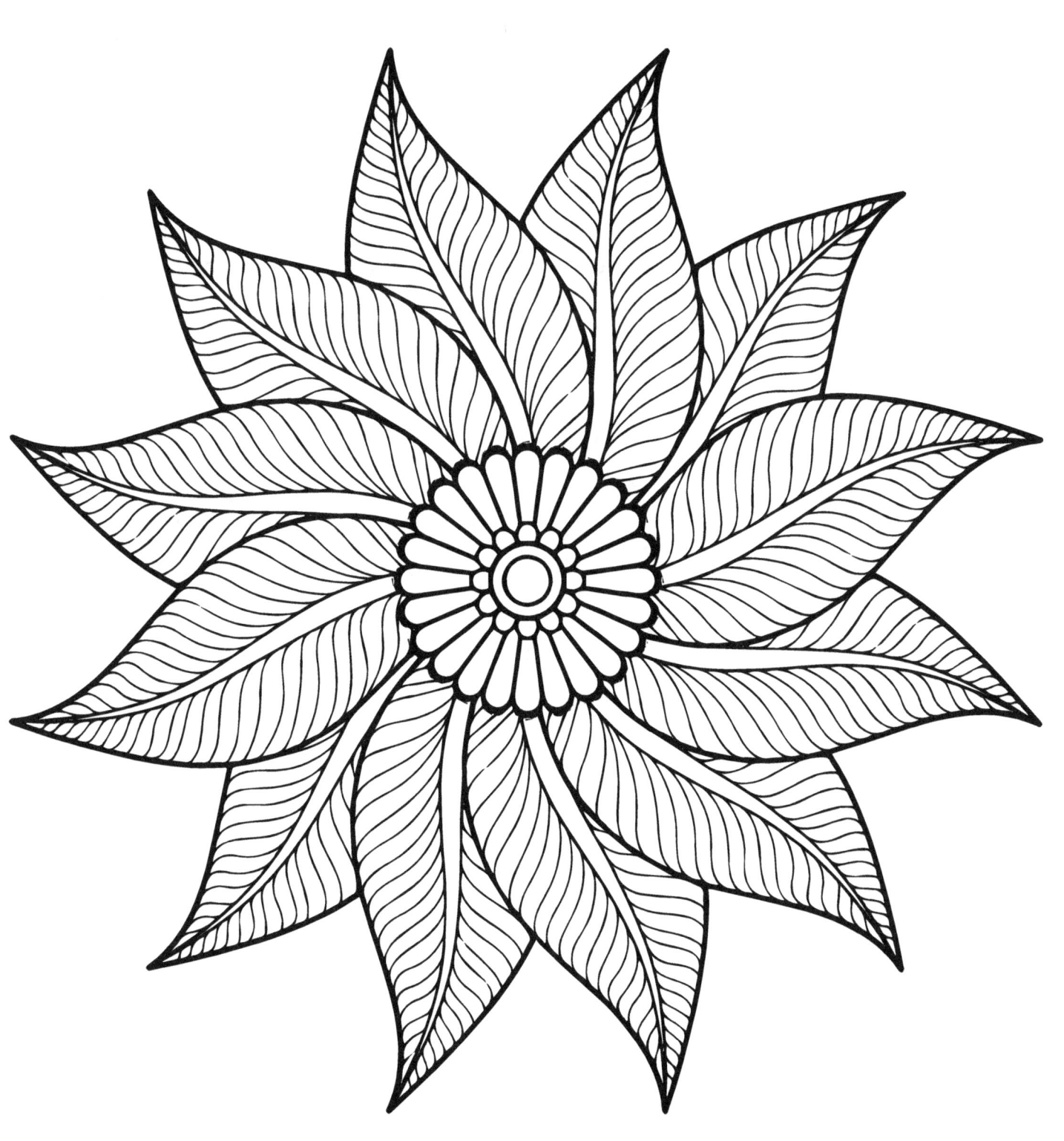

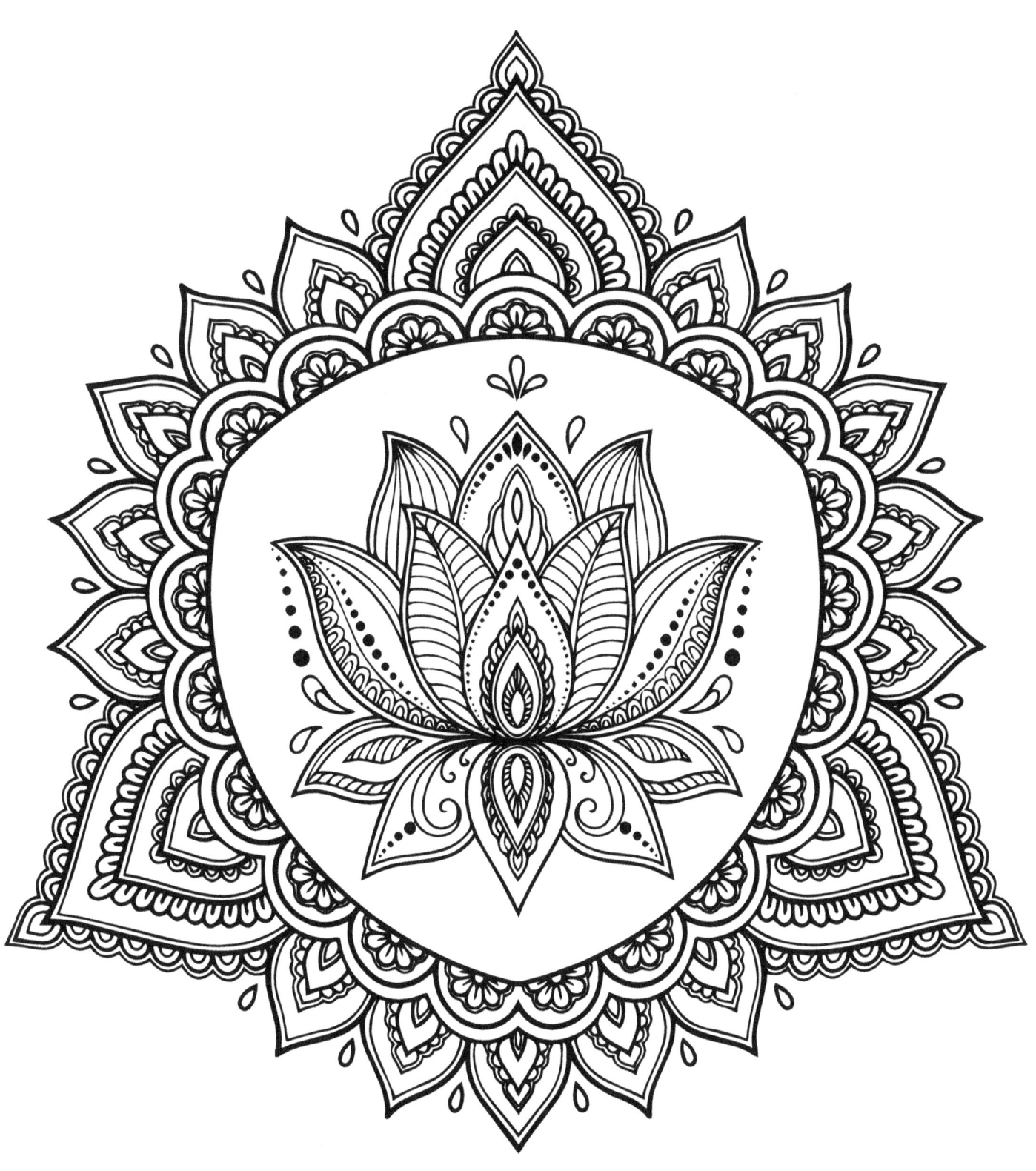

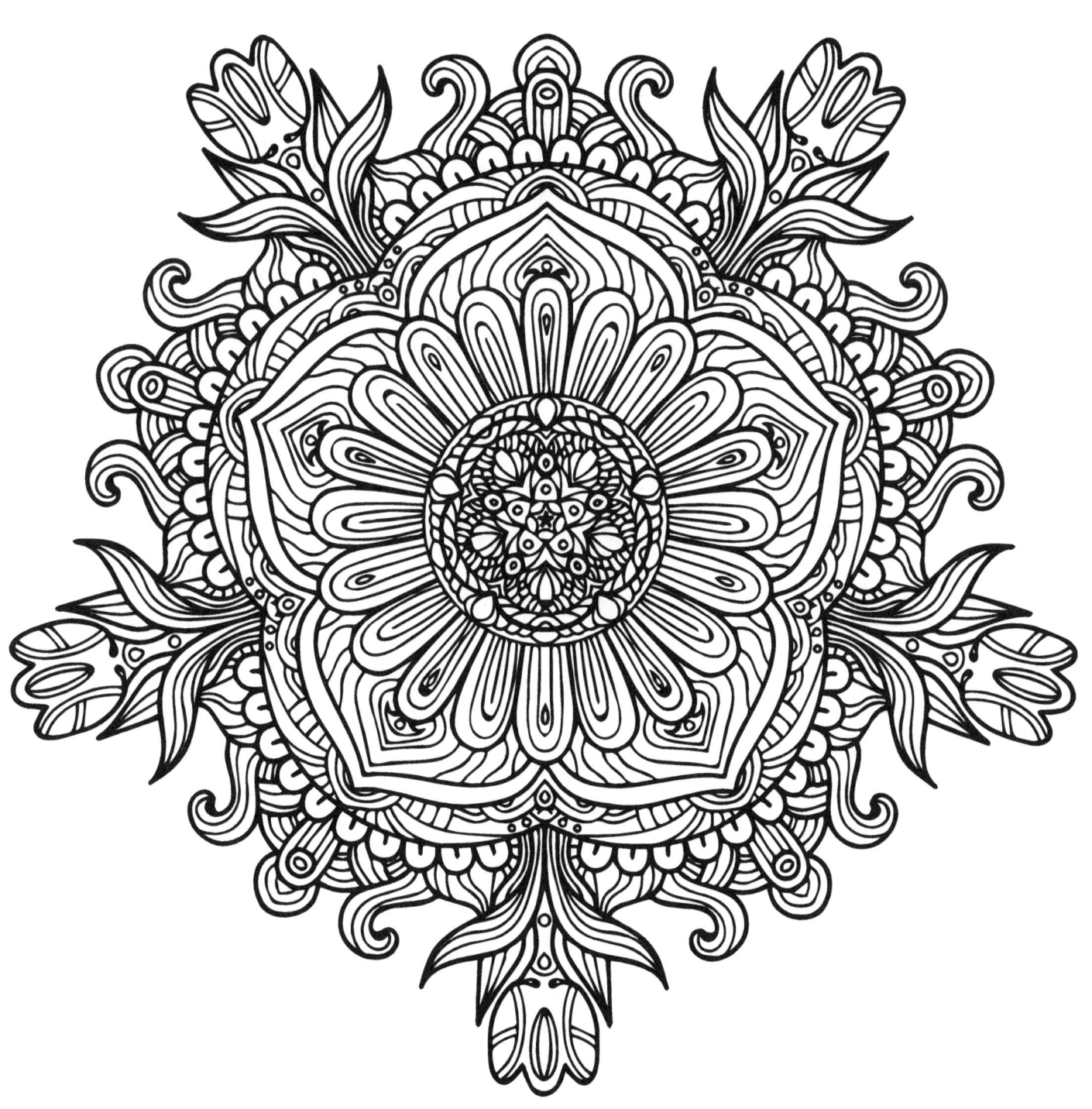

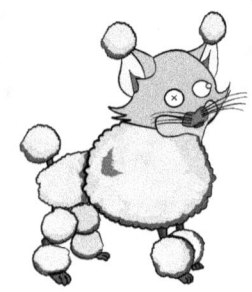

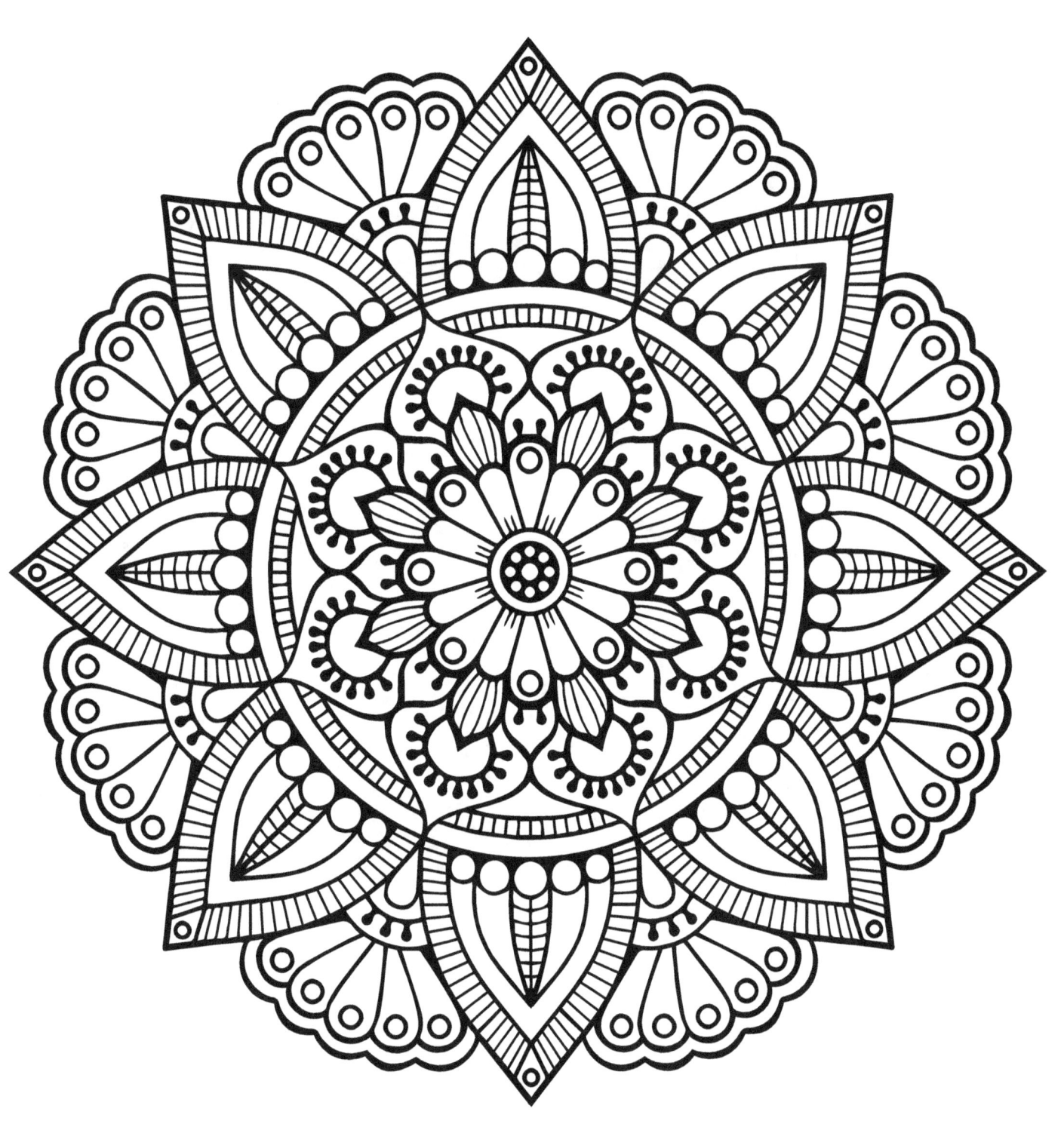

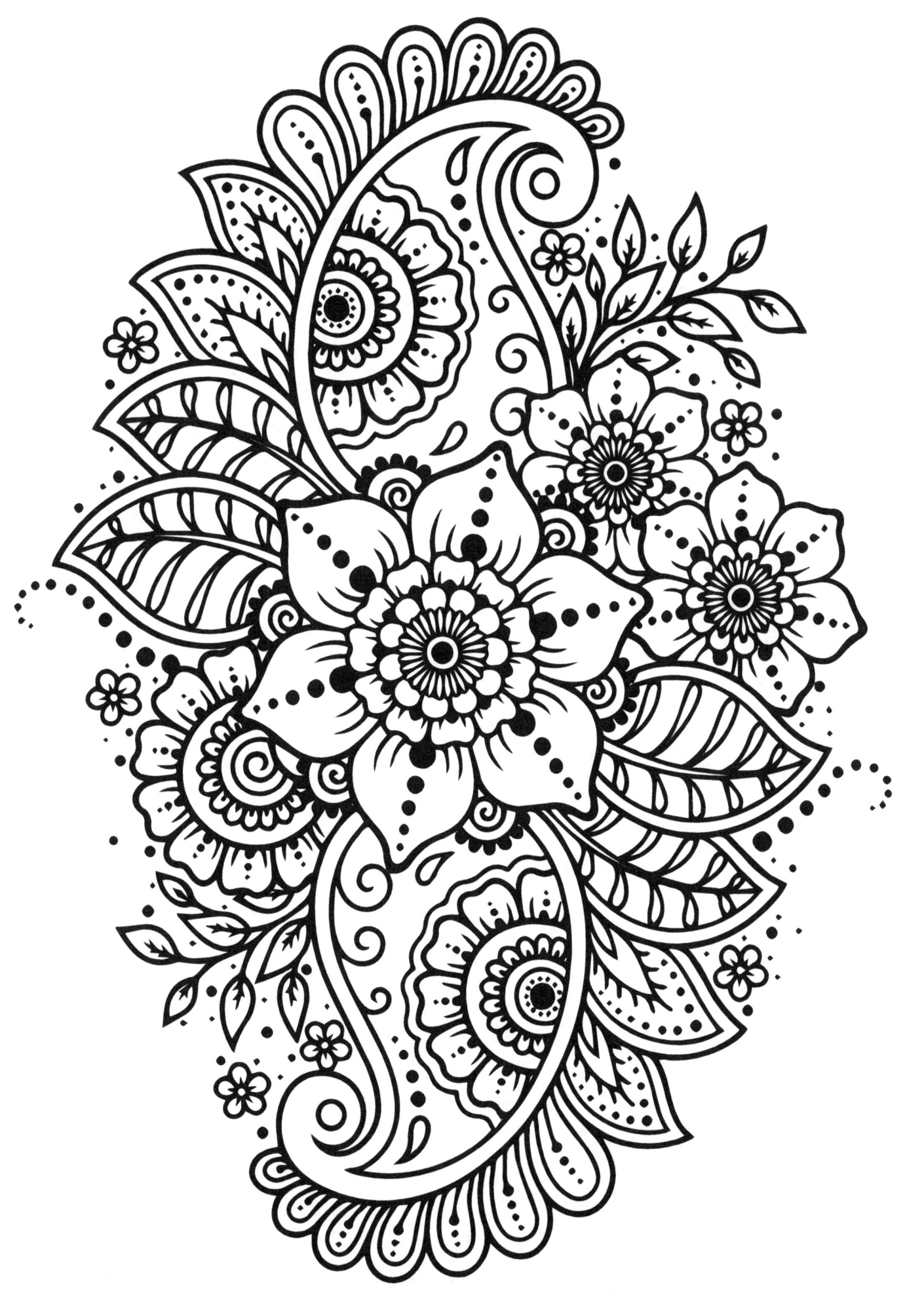

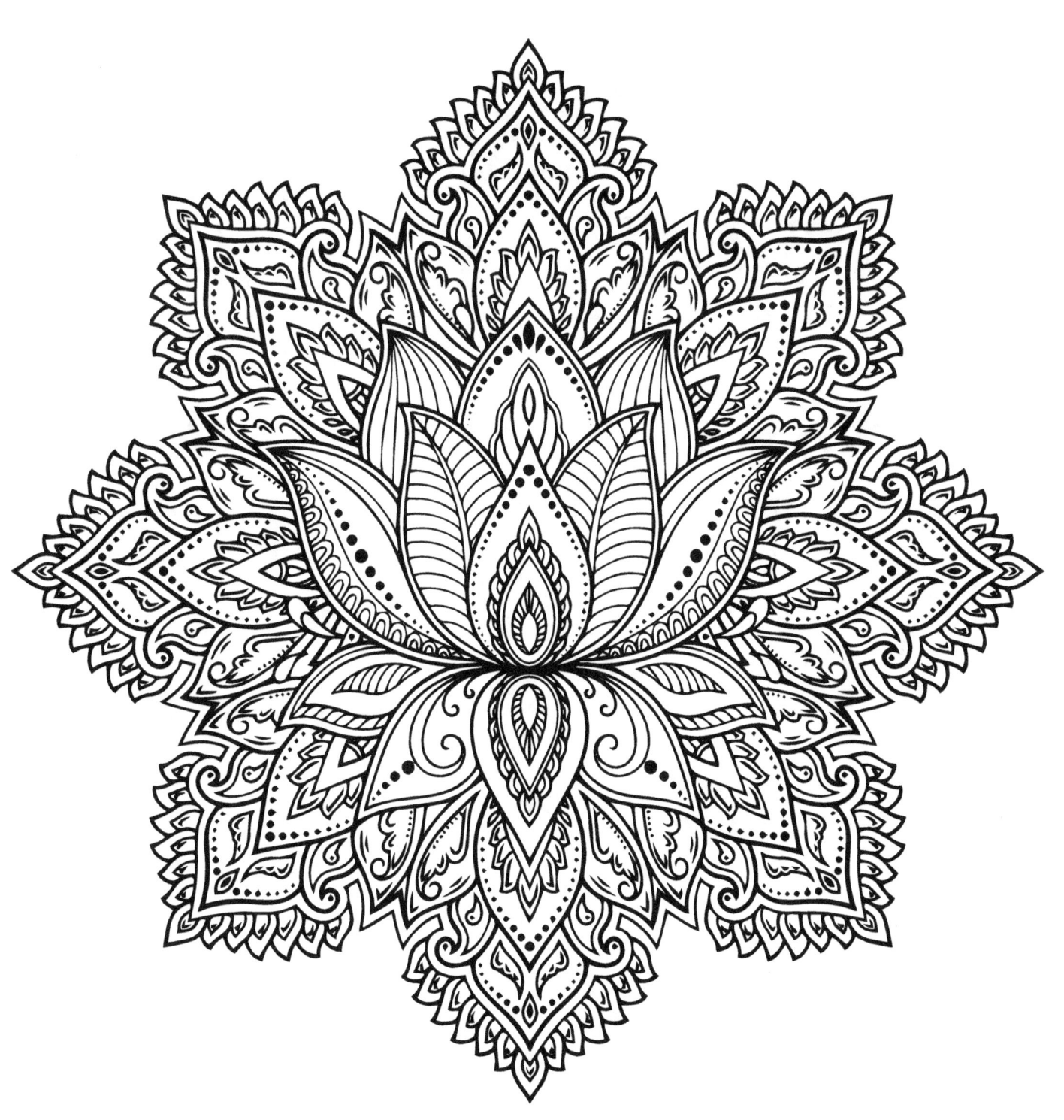

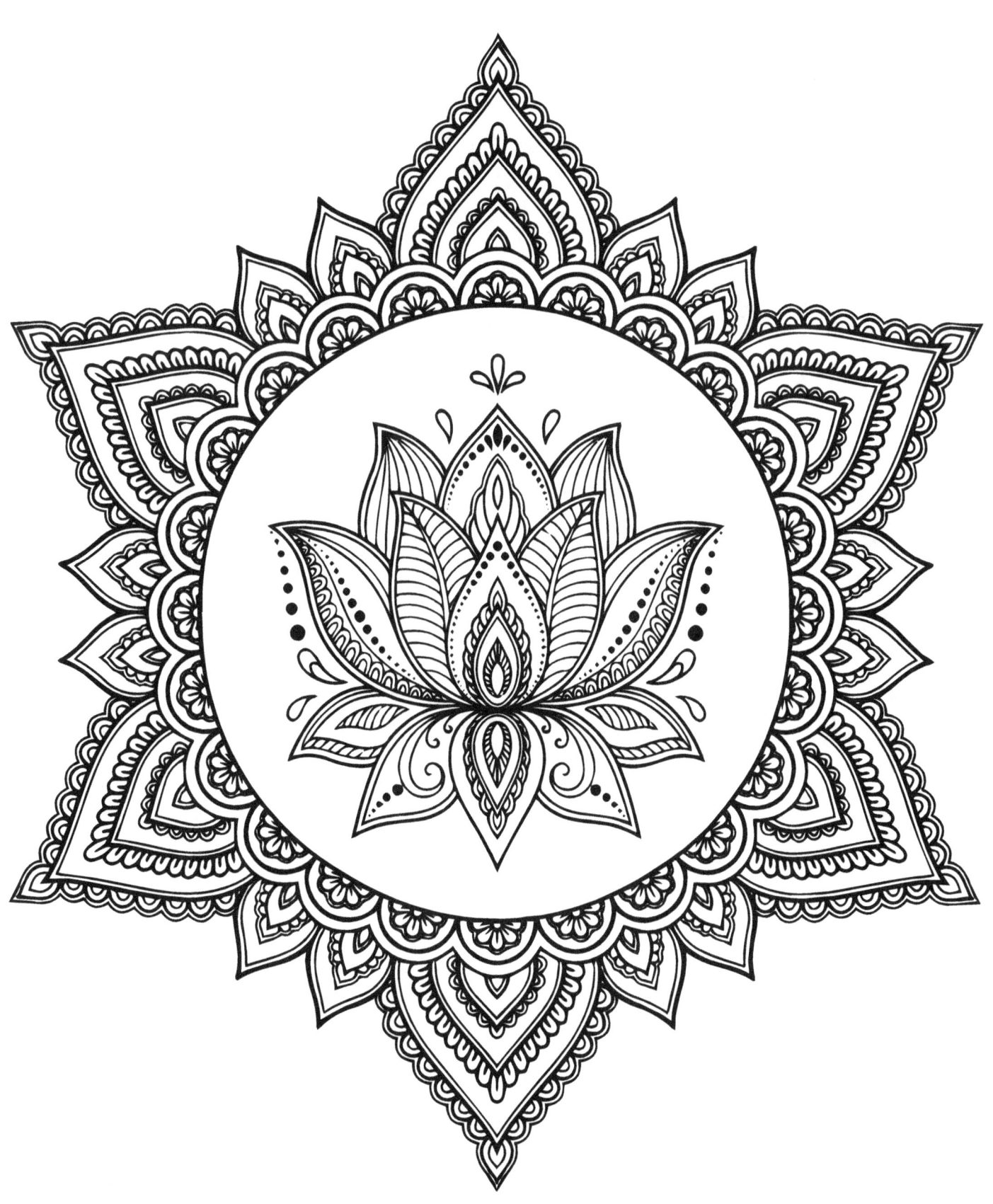

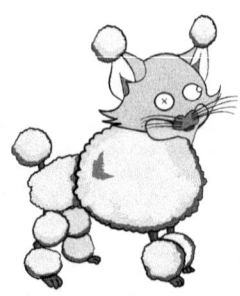

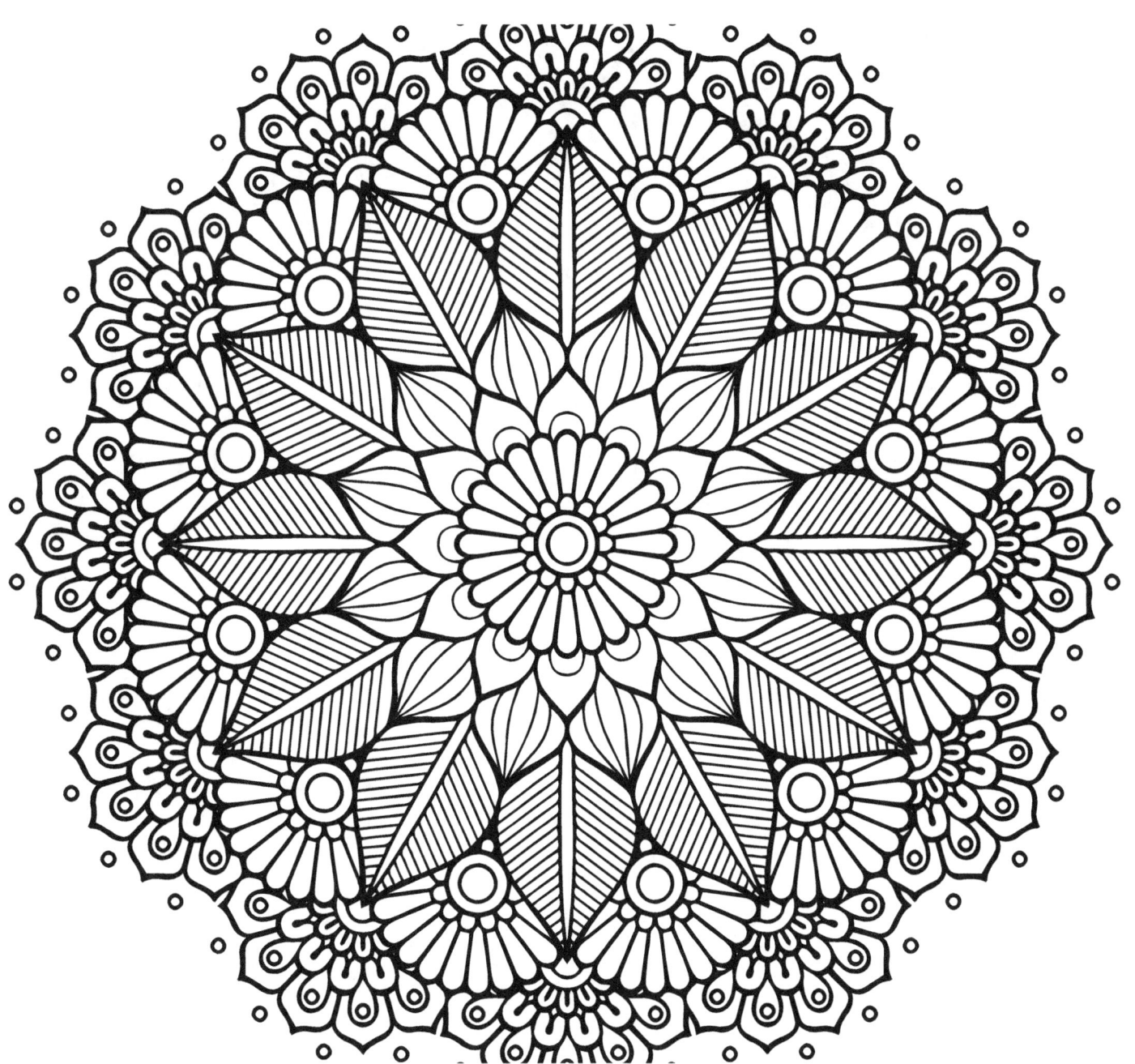